nshkabipple glow fis
n eye splash ck
cto fish food ul
ish upon a star gumbo
n presley singing blue
osmic tuna over sush
l what's black and white
? catfish tales beach
vang chung-waterworld
splash the laguna tuna
l bonds heart and sole
perstarfish rolly polly
the koi sea blackened
l bluegill recycle for the
enemom one fish, two
kissing fish ray of hope

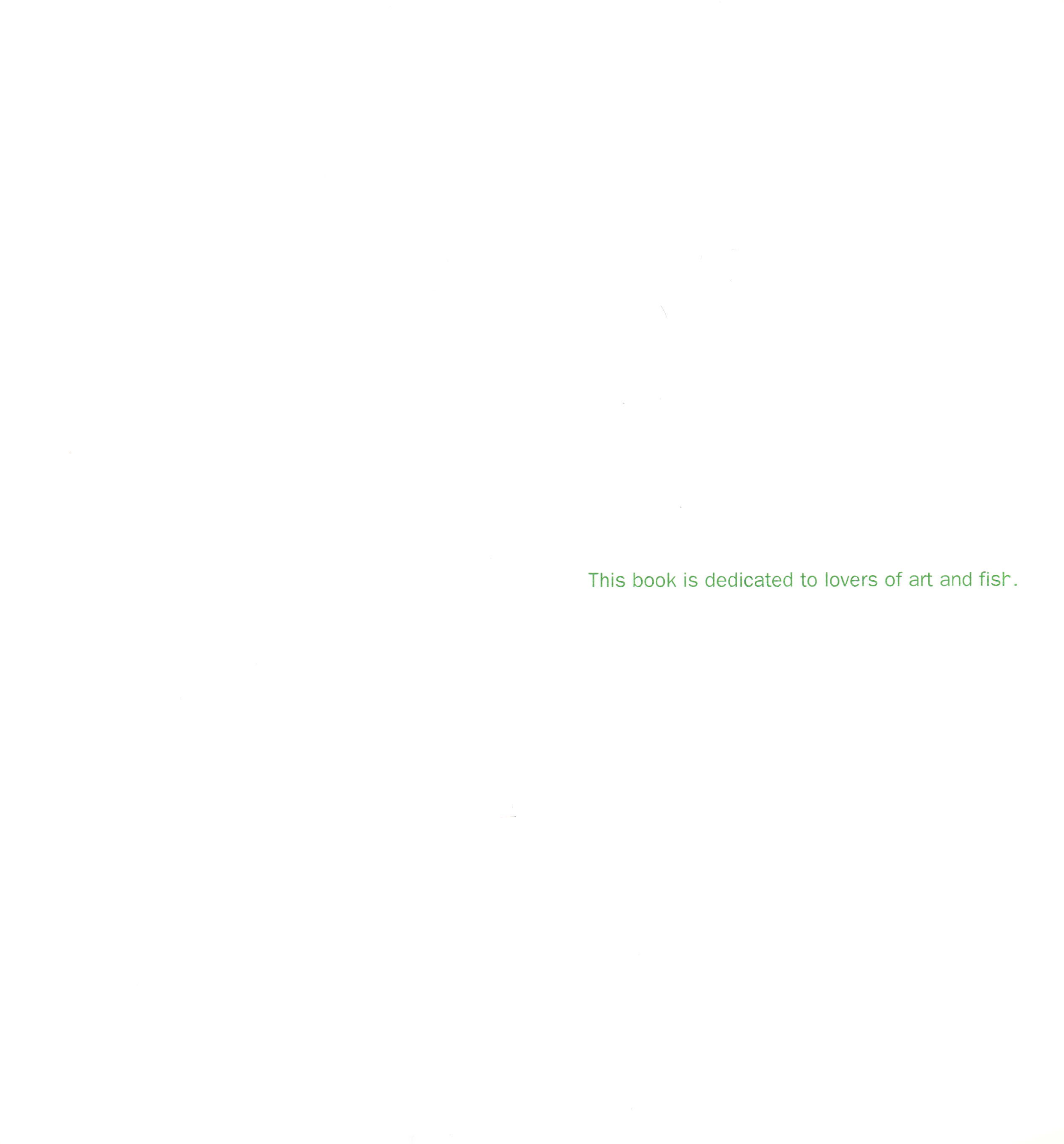

This book is dedicated to lovers of art and fish.

book info stuff

GoFish!: The Offishial Tale

ISBN 0-9709282-0-3

Written by: Vanessa Weibler Paris

Designed by: Jody DeAngelo Farrell

Photography by: Denise Keim

First Edition: October 2001

Printed by: MailWell Print Group

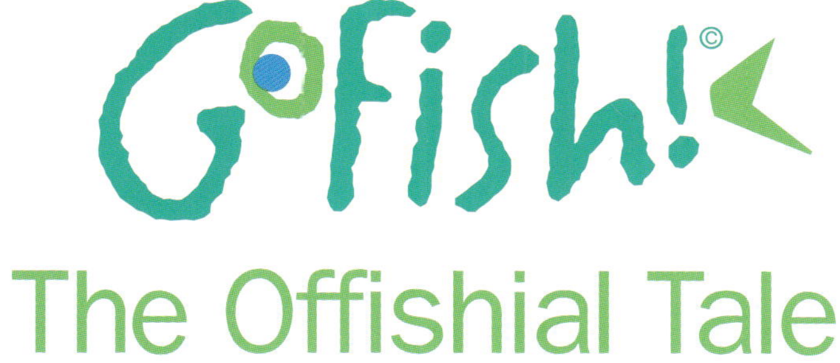
GoFish!©
The Offishial Tale

tableofcontents

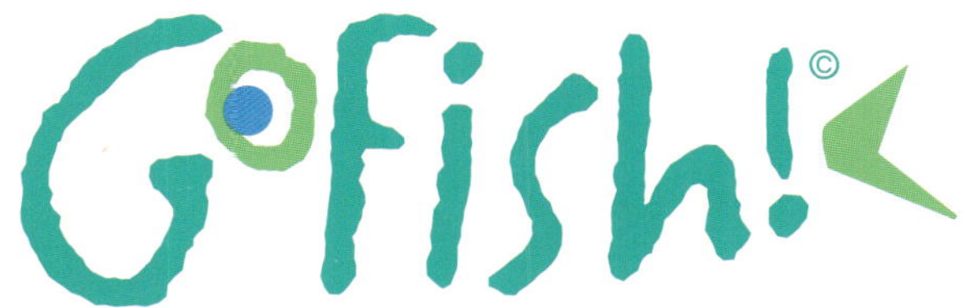

Many people have come to regard art as something for others, something that is found only in museums, and which often cannot be understood. GoFish! steps beyond all that.

Despite the fact that many of the fish sculptures incorporate sophisticated references to art, history, politics and science, no one feels excluded by them. People love to talk about their favorite fish, the funniest fish, the most amazing fish, the stupidest fish. It's okay that everyone is a critic, because everyone is an art lover. It's okay to talk about art, because it's interesting, and it's funny, and it's not hard to understand.

This project has produced results that happily exceed those envisioned by its organizers. The enthusiasm with which the community has embraced the effort has surprised even its earliest supporters—PNC Financial Services Group and National City Bank, who stepped forward as major sponsors, and the City of Erie, whose mayor and council continue to be among its strongest boosters. And even the Fish Commish, the committee that has been responsible for all the numerous details of the project, has been somewhat overwhelmed by the public's amazingly positive response. GoFish! speaks to an inborn impulse in all of us—a natural and enthusiastic response to art. We hope GoFish! will remind people that art is an important part of human life.

In the summer of 2001, art took the form of a fish. But there are many forms of art—music and literature, sculpture and theater. So be inspired by GoFish! and take advantage of all that Erie's arts community has to offer. Enjoy our museums and galleries, theaters and concert halls. And remember that art really *is* for everyone.

John Vanco, Director, Erie Art Museum
August 2001

“Hey, I have an idea. How about we put gigantic fish all over downtown Erie?”

Absurd? Well, it might have been, if Erie wasn't the city it is. When Susan Black-Keim, Gannon University's vice president for university advancement, proposed the idea to put on a public art extravaganza modeled after Chicago's successful Cows on Parade,™ our community was immediately hooked. And **GoFish!** was born.

A volunteer committee— which dubbed itself the Fish Commish — came together in fall of 2000. Mary Alice Doolin, teacher and longtime supporter of Gannon, and Jody Farrell, creative director at Tungsten Creative Group, agreed to serve as co-chairs. The Commish began planning, and addressing the questions— hundreds! perhaps thousands!— that needed answers in order to make GoFish! a success. **How would we create the fish models? Who would support the project? Which local artists would share in something unlike anything that had ever been done here before?**

Two different fish models, horizontal and vertical, a combination of sunfish and cartoon fish, were designed by local artist David L. Seitzinger. They were cast at MFG, a Union City fiberglass company. And PNC Financial Services Group and National City Bank showed their support by stepping up to become corporate sponsors.

The questions continued. **Who would sponsor the fish? Who would convert them into works of art? Where would they be stored?**

Potential sponsors were contacted, including companies, organizations, individuals and groups of individuals. An application process for artists was put in place. A storage space in the Avalon Hotel was procured and christened The Hatchery.

The waters of GoFish! began to bubble. Sponsors were snatching up fish as eagerly as a hungry perch would a juicy worm. And, in April, the first fish— Blackened Whitefish, a creation of David N. Seitzinger (son of the sculptor)— was released from Erie's cozy pond into a larger and more crowded lake. (As a follow-up to their 1998 initiative, Chicago had invited other cities to send one of their sculptures for a special "City Critters" summer round-up at Lincoln Park Zoo.)

As winter thawed into spring, artists began receiving their raw fish to transform. And the very first local GoFish! fish, Bill Doan's Cosmic Fish, was installed in front of Gannon's Old Main on May 2, 2001. Then, as spring began to warm into summer, the fish began breaking the water's surface, turning up all over the place.

And now, the questions weren't just being asked by the committee — they were being asked by the whole community. **How'd that one get cut into pieces? How'd they get that fish all the way up there? Which one's your favorite? When will the next ones be installed? Hey, here's my camera—will you take my picture next to it?**

As the greater downtown area was transformed into a virtual aquarium, Erieites became inspired by the art and unleashed their own creativity, prompting yet another question: **is there no *end* to the seemingly infinite fish puns that our clever community could conjure up?** (We're hooked on GoFish!...we're up to the gills in fish...this project is fin-tastic...things are coming along swimmingly...we've been lured in by all the colorful creatures. And now, you're even reading *GoFish!: The Offishial Tale*.)

Well, the answer to that question is yet to be seen, as the fish have become so beloved to Erie that they will forever be in our memories and our imaginations, long after the fish not retained by sponsors are auctioned off at the Fish Market in October.

But in the reminiscence of all the rallying together, in the afterglow of the exhilration, in the wake of all the wonderful memories we'll have of the summer of 2001, it's only appropriate that the many, *many* questions evoked have an answer with a single, strong, spirited exclamation point: **GoFish!**

Proceeds of GoFish! benefit Gannon University's Scholarship Fund and the Erie Public Art Fund of The Erie Art Museum.

eriefishhistory

1795
Pioneers located on Presque Isle and had to fish from their log canoes to get food. All varieties of lake fish were abundant, particularly black bass[1].

1815
Erie's first commercial fisherman, a recluse named McKinney, choked to death on a fish bone.

1830
Prior to this year, all Lake Erie fish were caught with a hook and line. The first Seine (net) fishermen were David Fowzier, Thomas Horton, William Buckingham and Abraham Huntsbarger.

1850
The first pound net[2] was used on Lake Erie.

1852
Captain Nash caught the first white fish on Lake Erie.

1854
Prior to this year, sturgeon[3] were considered useless. When they were caught, they were taken to the peninsula and buried.

1872
The first pound nets were set off the port of Erie to catch several tons of sturgeon. The roe was removed, salted, and sent to Germany to be prepared as caviar.

1882
The steamer Frank Mattison—the first one owned at Erie's port—was built and launched.[4]

1885
The Erie State Hatchery was opened at the corner of 2nd and Sassafras[5] Streets.

1892
This year, 12,786,579[6] fish were caught in Lake Erie.

1894
This year, about a million more fish were caught than the year previous[7].

1895
The Erie Yacht Club opened.

1896
Prominent local anglers[8] who guarded their favcrite fishing spots jealously included Rev. Wm. Flint, Dr. H.A. Spencer, John Banyard, Tom Crowley, Wm. L. Scott, Tim Lynch, Alfred King, John P. Vincent, J. Ross Thompson, Jake Graham, John C. Hilton, J.H. McCracken, Sam Woods, Frank Grant, John Dodge and Fred Knobloch[9].

[1] Also known as the smallmouth bass, brown bass, green bass, redeye bass, Oswego bass, green trout, smallie, bronzeback, or Micropterus dolomieu

[2] A fish trap consisting of a netting arranged into a directing wing and an enclosure with a narrow entrance

[3] The word sturgeon, which is in the name of two GoFish! fish, rhymes with burgeon, durgin, spurgeon, spurgin, surgeon, turgeon, virgen, virgin and yeargin

[4] A completely different Frank Mattison directed the 1926 movie *Buffalo Bill on the U.P. Trail*

[5] Ground sassafras leaves are used as a thickening agent for gumbo and fish stews

[6] This number includes every numeral between one and nine except for three and four

[7] That would be approximately 13,786,579

[8] To angle is to fish with a hook

[9] In the latest Erie phone directory, there are listings for three Flints, 39 Spencers, eight Crowleys, 71 Scotts, 51 Lynches, 146 Kings, 17 Vincents, 193 Thompsons, 72 Grahams, one Hilton, 20 McCrackens, 31 Woodses, 24 Grants, seven Dodges and four Knoblochs...some of them inevitably descended from these fishing afishionados

thegofish!story

how to make art fun

One day, the spirit of Oliver Hazard Perry decided that there should be fish all over Erie.

(Nope. Wasn't that easy.)

So he snapped his fingers, spun around three times while chanting'*fishkabob-fishkabob-fishkabob*, and BAM! there they were.

(Uh uh. Wasn't that quick.)

And then he smiled, because Erie's streets were filled with bright, colorful fish, bringing happiness to the entire city, and he alone could take the credit.

(Bwahaha! As *if* it could've been done by one person...try dozens, even hundreds!)

how to turn the tide

Okay, so it wasn't our idea originally. Switzerland gets credit for the first public art project, and Chicago was right behind. But when Susan Black-Keim visited the city in fall 2000 and learned about their Cows on Parade™, she knew it *had* to happen here.

Phones started ringing. Susan approached Mary Alice Doolin, a longtime Gannon supporter, who spoke with Angela Brooks, a member of Gannon's communications staff, who spoke with Jody Farrell, a creative director at a local advertising agency, who spoke with a whole lot of people who were thrilled to come together and join a full committee. Mary Alice and Jody agreed to co-chair the effort. Oh— and while other cities have hired full-time paid staffs to oversee their projects, Erie's would be run entirely by volunteers.

The Fish Commish

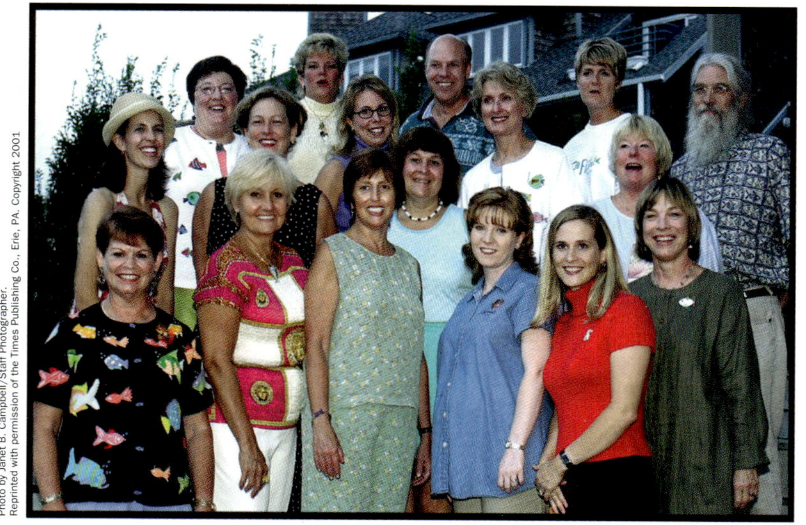

Photo by Janet B. Campbell/Staff Photographer.

how to swim with it

Cows. Pigs. Ringtailed lemurs. What did *they* have to do with Erie? No, the mascot had to be something symbolic, something meaningful to us all. So, since Erie is right on the lake *and* has the honor of once having been the world's largest freshwater fishing port, the theme of fish was chosen. A bunch of different names, such as FabFishFest, FishFestival and FishFetish were considered before the simple yet exclamatory GoFish! was agreed upon. And the committee decided to dub itself the Fish Commish.

One of the original fish sketches

In order to gain local support, we went straight to the top. Members of the Commish met with representatives of the City to talk logistics, clearances, and insurance, and Mayor Joyce Savocchio gave GoFish! her blessing. Things moved forward. The Fish Commish determined tentative locations for the fish, created a patron brochure and website, and developed the necessary contracts.

how to make it reel

David L. Seitzinger was lured in. Graduate of the Columbus College of Art & Design, degreed in industrial design, drawer, sculptor, former toy designer for Marx Toys, lifelong artist: David was a natural to get involved with bringing the fish from concept to reality.

The advice provided by other cities doing public art projects included "don't make it too big!" and

The original horizontal and vertical models

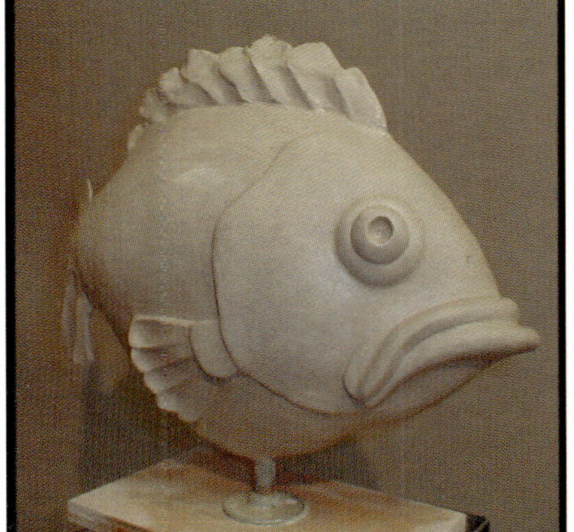

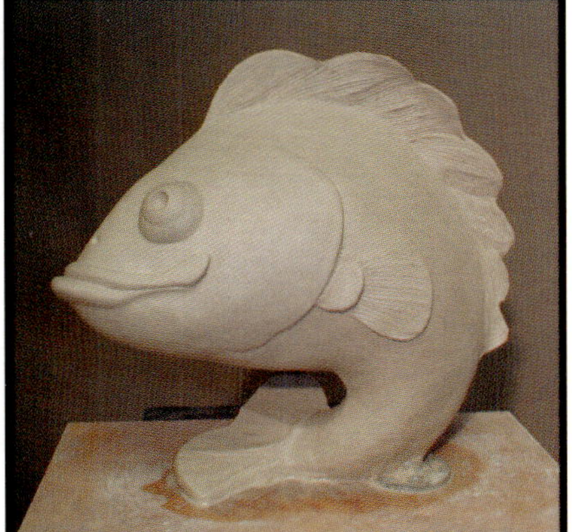

David L. Seitzinger, fish sculptor

"don't make more than one version!"—both of which David disregarded in bringing the GoFish! to life. He was determined to make it as good as Chicago's, or even better.

First, David did pencil sketches of what he imagined the fish would look like. His main goal was to make the fish artist-friendly; he wanted to provide them with a broad canvas upon which to create, with lots of smooth surfaces. Of David's three initial designs, the Commish chose two for production—one vertical and one horizontal. He made clay models of each, about 16 inches long. He then constructed two full-size fish skeletons of plywood. This was done by taking detailed measurements of the models, transferring them to paper and enlarging each view to full size. From the paper patterns, David then cut and formed the plywood and applied plaster of paris, sculpting the fish form—at six by four feet and one hundred pounds—creating each entire fish from which fiberglass molds were manufactured.

A local company, Union City-based Molded Fiber Glass Companies (MFG), signed on to manufacture the fish, and Horton Precast Concrete of Girard would produce the bases. The Avalon Hotel agreed to loan some of its storage space for the fish to be stored, and the area was christened the Hatchery. Howard Industries gave us a great deal on plaques for the bases. And Star Mobile Homes Supply offered—free of charge!—to drive back and forth from MFG to Erie each Monday, delivering newly-cast fish in a truck that could hold only ten.

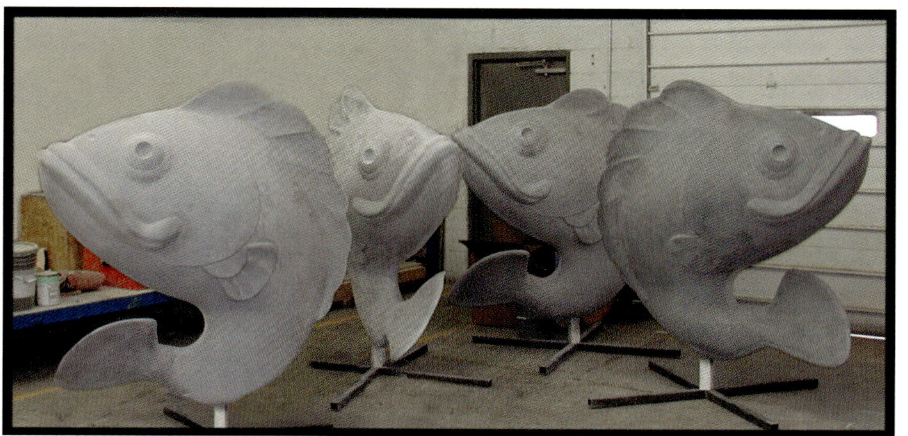

"Naked" fish at Molded Fiber Glass Companies

Seemingly endless logistical questions were addressed—what materials to use, what kind of paint and varnish would work best, how to secure each fish to its base, how to mount the plaques on the base. Many things were figured out as we went along, relying upon the companies' expertise and, in a number of cases, letting them work things out together.

how to go with the flow

A mid-December launch party featured two fish models and acquainted many local businesses with GoFish! Soon after, The PNC Financial Services Group and National City signed on as major sponsors of the project, and fish sales were underway.

In mid-January, an artists' meeting was held, during which MFG shared product specs, let them know what could and couldn't be used on

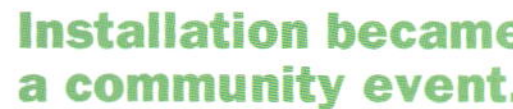

Installation became a community event.

the fish, answered questions, and received input and suggestions from the artists themselves.

Interested artists were asked to submit sketches, resumes and portfolios, resulting in a list of 150 artists from which sponsors could choose. GoFish! set up a relationship with Golden Artist Colors, from which artists could order two different "fish kits." One included primary paint colors, and the other contained primer, adhesives, and other products to texturize the fish.

At the same time, potential patrons were being contacted, many agreeing to purchase a fish— either to be sold at the Fish Market Auction in October or, for a slightly higher cost, to be retained by the patron. And the Fish Commish contacted businesses located on proposed fish sites, letting them know the fish were coming.

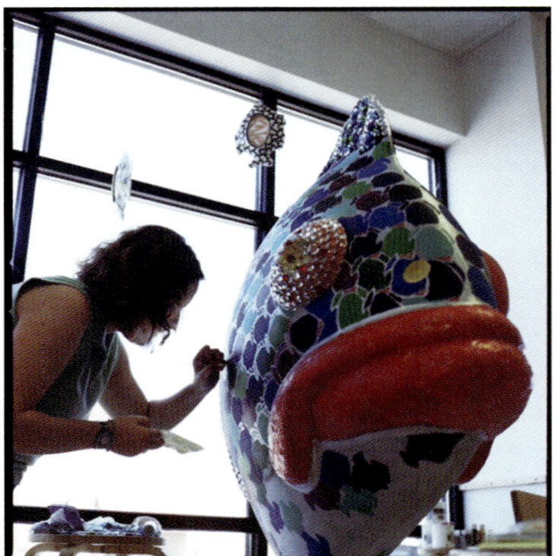

By mid-summer, 95 fish had been hatched. Artists were turning the naked fiberglass into wonderful, whimsical works of art that were, school by school, flooding the streets of downtown Erie.

Kate McCune-Nash at work on Bouillabaisse

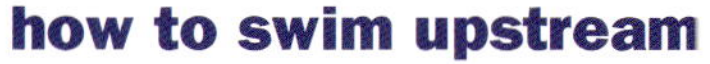

how to swim upstream

Troubleshooting, problem-solving and rolling with the punches became a typical workday for the Fish Commish.

There were waves. The first batch of fish, for instance, didn't have the right pole, and the design needed to be altered before manufacturing any more. While the original intent was for all the fish to be located downtown, sponsor requests and other circumstances prompted several fish to be placed in outlying areas. And then, of course, the Sturgeon General went missing.

Fishmania abounds.

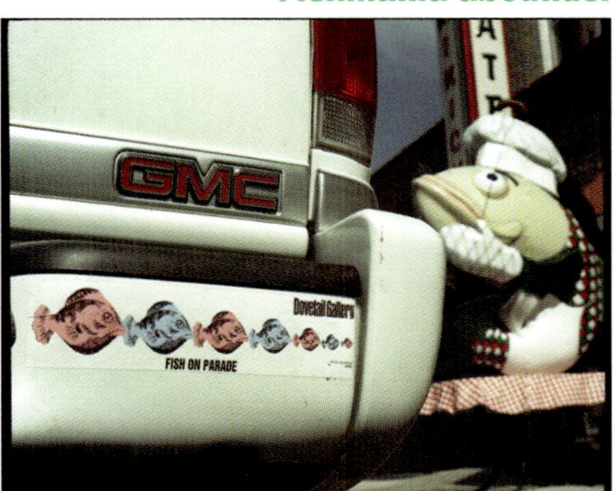

But, all in all, the whole process went swimmingly. Everything came together— a volunteer committee that swapped the blood in their veins for lake water, vendors willing to swim the extra mile, patrons eager to take the bait, artists ready to dive right in, and a community of people who would open their souls and their imaginations and fall in love with the fish— to make GoFish! a splashing success.

“gofish!”

Night Swimming
artist: Shelle Barron
patron: Molded Fiber Glass Companies
location: Dobbins Landing

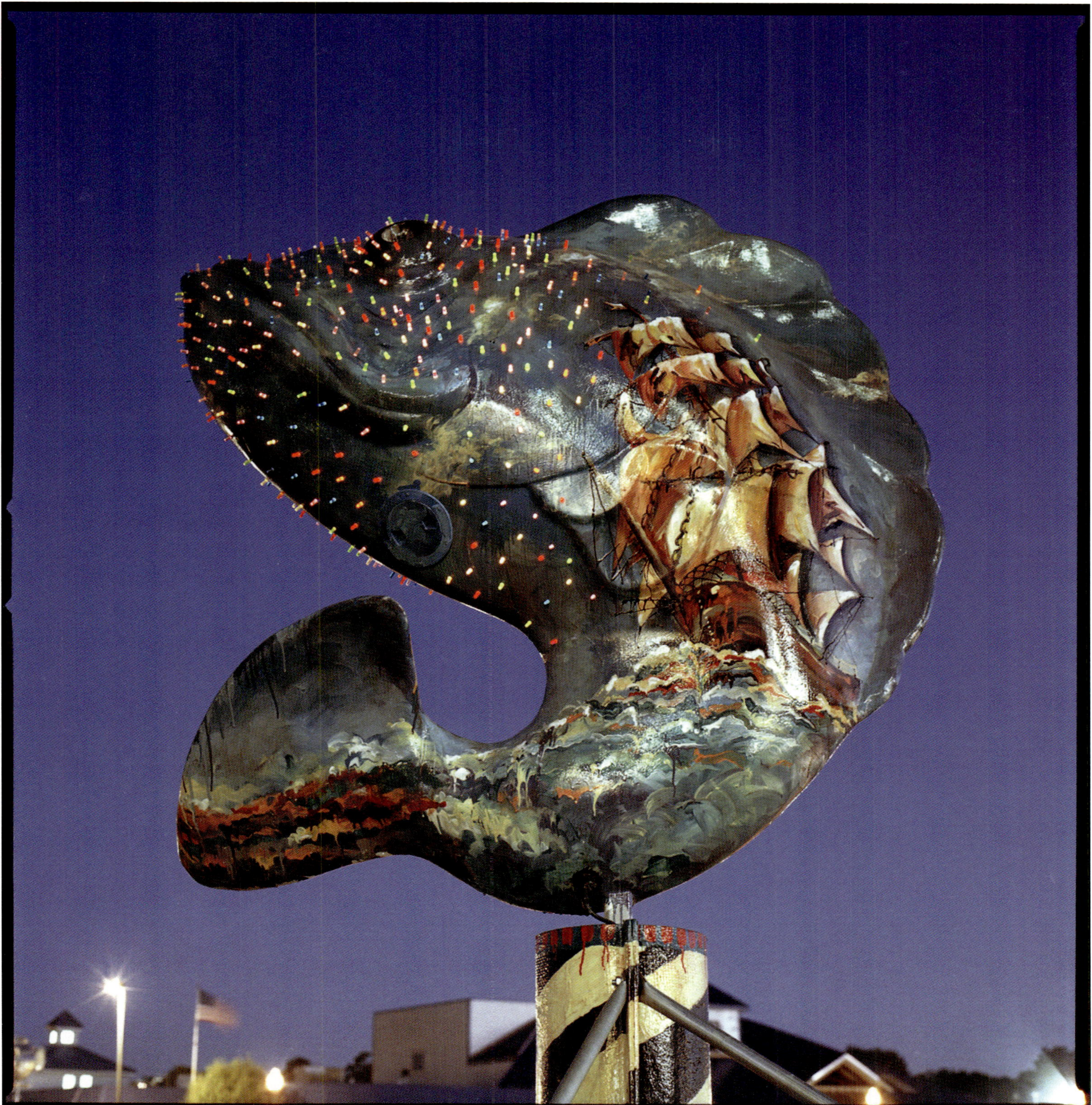

"The first fish I ever touched was 'Red & White & Bluegill' at Dobbins Landing on a bright sunny day with my cousin from Missouri, my mom, and my two sisters. We were going to go up the tower when I spotted the fish and asked if we could go touch it. I walked over to it and touched it. It felt bumpy and cold. Then I tried to kiss it on the lips, but I was too short! Now I love touching all the GoFish. They are great and really neat to see."

Christina Wendel

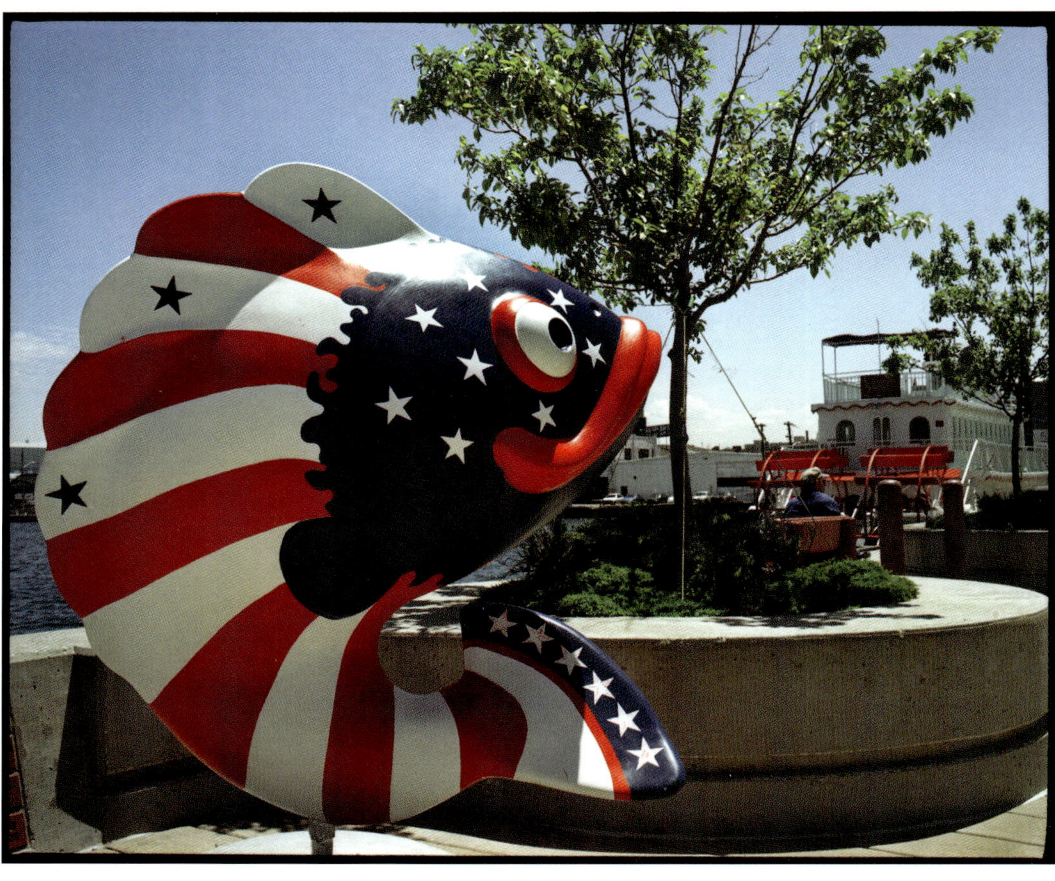

Red & White & Bluegill
artists: Walnut Creek Middle School Art Students
patron: The Vicary Family
location: Dobbins Landing

"I was one of the many children that had worked on The Red and White and Bluegill. And let me say this...we had worked so hard in two weeks on that fish, we all were dedicated and focused on making the fish look professional. It made us feel special when we looked at the finished product. The hardest part was making it look good enough to pass as the same or maybe better than a fish that an artist had made. I almost looked at it as a competion to see who could look the best. All the kids from Walnut Creek Middle School who had worked on The Red and White and Bluegill had an awesome time, but we also looked at it as a challenge. We couldn't let it get sloppy or make it look like kids made it. Well, we all had a good time and made new friends during this exciting two weeks!" — Kayla Wykoff

Wang Chung-Waterworld
artist: Ron Bayuzick
patron: In Loving Memory of Ron Holstein
location: 411 State Street

Filet Award
A real metamorphosis

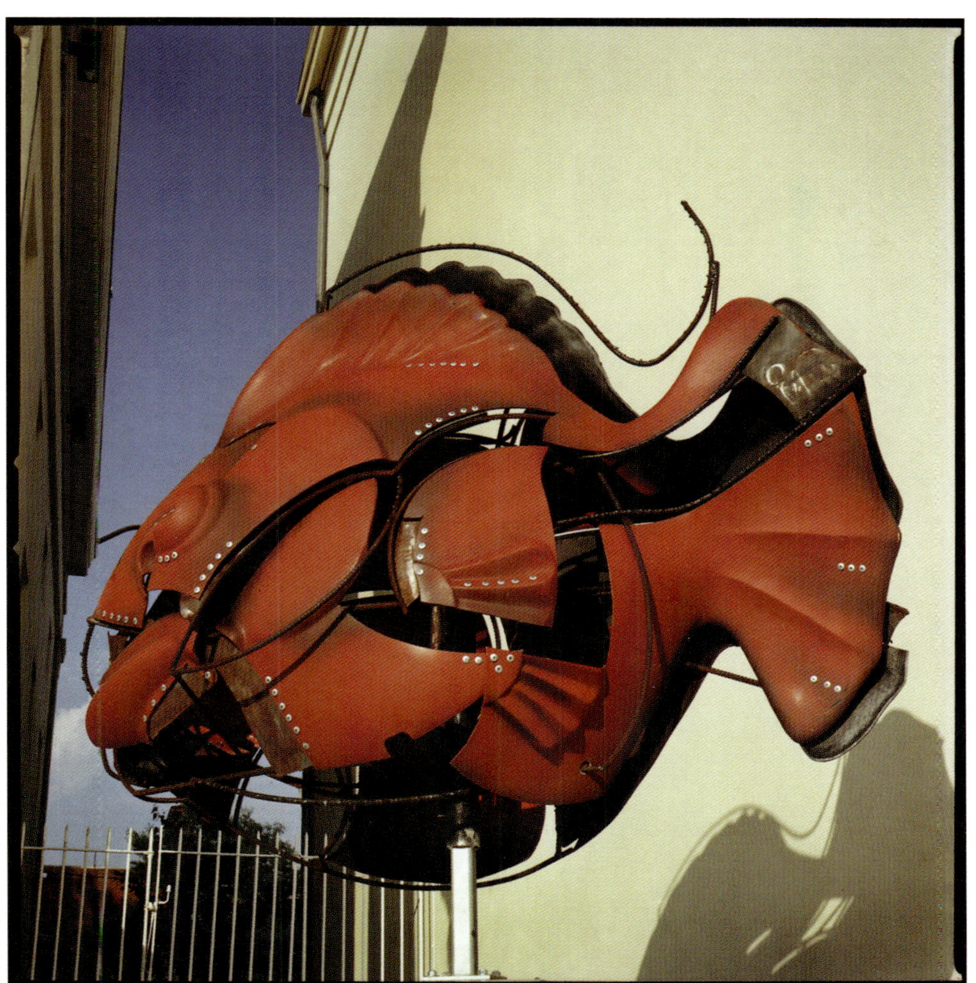

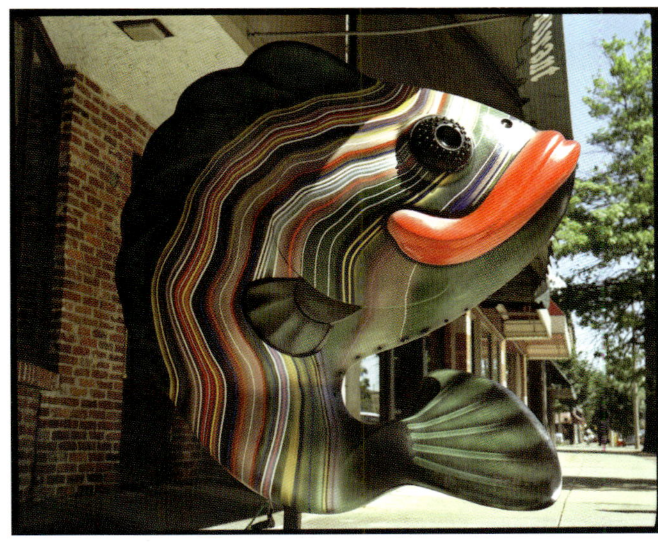

Lilly the Lip
artists: Rick & Susan James
patron: Plymouth Tavern
location: 1109 State Street

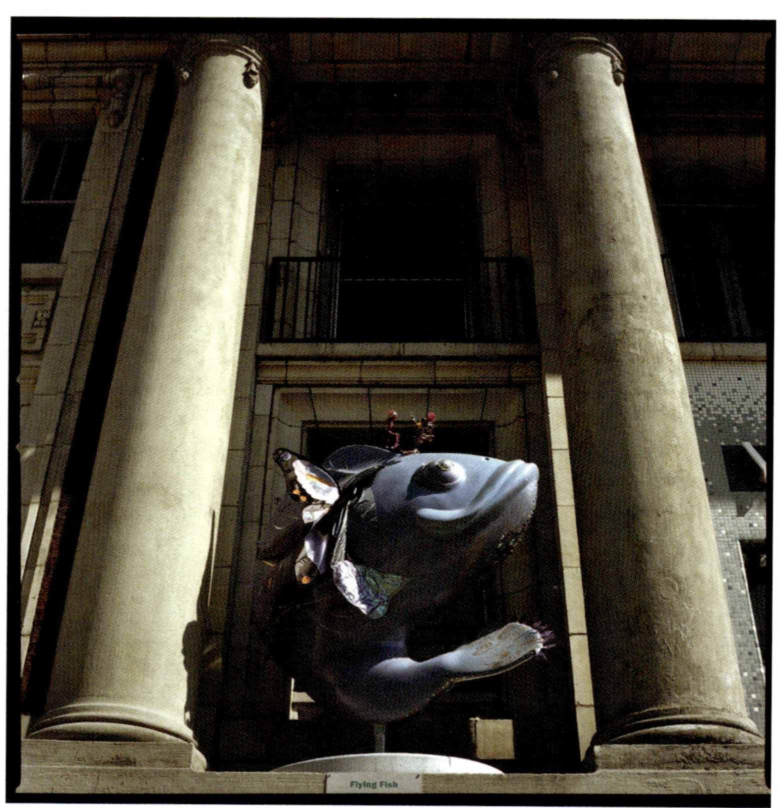

Flying Fish
artist: Carol Posch Comstock
patron: Greater Erie YMCA
location: West 10th & Peach Streets

agirlandherfish

Carol Posch Comstock has been a YMCA member for many years, so she was delighted when they chose her to design their fish.

She was so thrilled, in fact, that her original list had more than 100 ideas. She managed to narrow it down to 30, and then zeroed in on Flying Fish, the name of a level in children's swim classes.

As purple is her favorite color, Carol used many shades of violet and lilac. She worked on it for nearly seven weeks, every single day, and took so many photos that "it's like a boring baby album."

After it was installed, separation anxiety set in. Carol would suddenly think, "Oh, I haven't seen my fish for a week!" But doing a quick drive-by would bring relief— seeing the wings in motion made it feel alive to her, and "it's so happy when it's flying."

As an additional tribute, for the kickoff event, Carol wore clothing to match the fish, as well as a pin she made herself— a miniature Flying Fish.

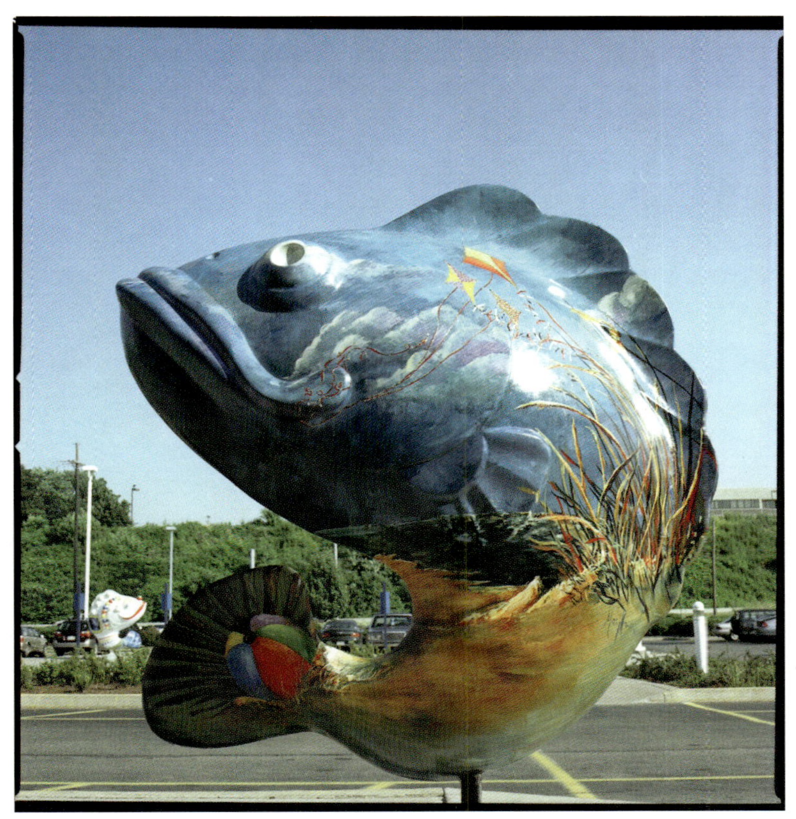

Beachin
artist: Mary L. Hamilton
patron: GPU Energy
location: 160 East Front Street

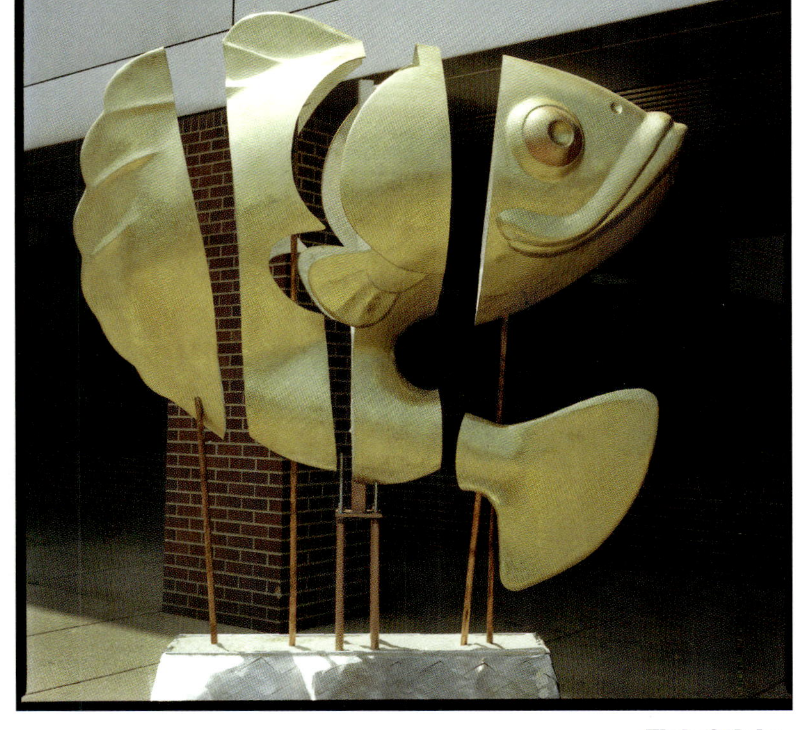

Fish Sticks
built by: Weber Murphy Fox Staff
designed by: Rich Speicher & Jeff Lander
patron: Weber Murphy Fox
location: 3rd & State Streets

"I was trying to decide what to have for dinner and

Bouillabaisse
artist: Kate McCune-Nash
patrons: Barbara Boddy & Donald Salwoski
location: 1011 State Street

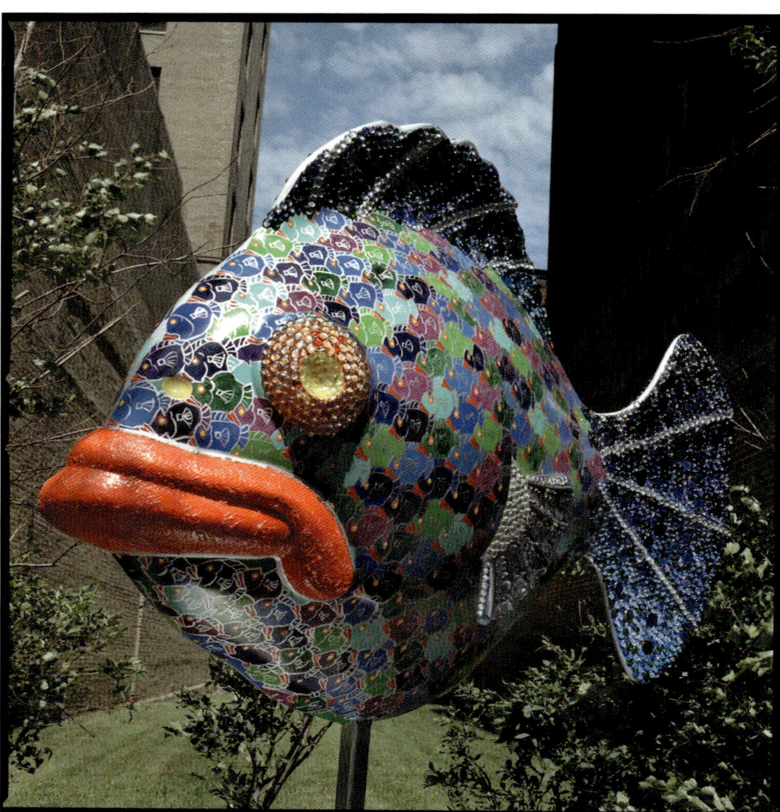

makeyourownbouillabaisse

- 3 lbs. of fish (any combination of eel, haddock, red snapper, bass, monkfish, etc.), cut into bite-sized pieces
- 3 lbs. lobster, broken into pieces
- 3 dozen mussels, washed and beards removed
- 3 leeks, slivered
- 2 onions, chopped
- 3 garlic cloves, minced
- 3 tomatoes, peeled, seeded and chopped
- 1/3 cup olive oil
- bouquet garni of thyme, bay leaf, parsley, and rosemary
- meaty pinch of saffron, heated and crumbled
- salt and pepper
- cayenne
- garnish: croutons fried in garlic-flavored oil

Heat the oil in a Dutch oven and add leeks, onions, garlic, and tomatoes— cooking over a low heat for at least 15 minutes. Add the bouquet garni and the heavy pieces of fish— cook gently for about 5 minutes. Add the remaining fish, lobster, and saffron and cover with water (or fish stock). Season with salt, pepper, and cayenne, and bring to a boil. Cook over medium heat for 10 minutes, then add the mussels and cook until they open their shells.

When ready to serve, strain the ingredients into a serving dish then pour the hot broth over top. Serve the croutons separately.

rove past

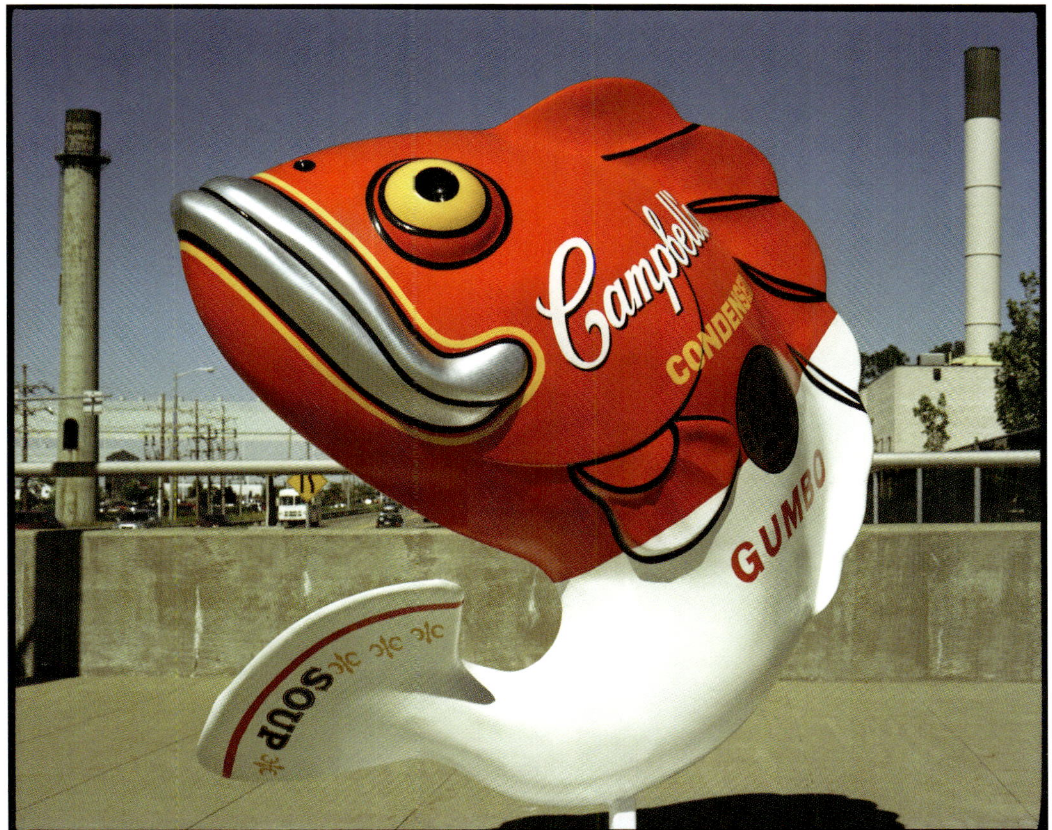

Gumbo
artists: fishtank creative
patron: fishtank creative
location: State Street & Bayfront Highway
People's Choice
3rd Place

...then the idea came to me."

Michelle Agens

I wish everyone would clean up the earth and their attitude. *J., 10* • I wish I didn't have to ceep mooving. *Joe, 9* • I wish that someday there would be a Christmas tree in my house. *Anthony, 6* • I wish the whole world would be nicer to each other. *A'londe, 9* • I wish older people would believe in younger people. *Marissa, 11* • I wish for no one in the hole world to be pore. *Tyree* • I wish the whole world was free not just America. *Joe, 9* • I wish that I didn't have to move every time I get comfortable. *Joseph, 9* • I wish everyone would respect each other. *Kayla, 9* • I wish there was no such things as drugs. *Rhonda, 13* • I wish that people would stop poluting the earth. *Briana, 8* • I wish there was no violence in this world. I wish I could have a big hug. *Noah, 12* • I wish my mom and dad were back together. I wish I could meet my family. I wish my mom would stop crying because my dad won't pick me up in the summer. *Teaira, 8* • I wish all the violence would stop. I wish mothers would stop leaving their children in their homes by themselves. I wish that people would stop going to bars and stop fighting and shooting each other. *Desire, 12* • I wish that when I grow up I could get a good education and be a teacher and a good life and a house with my family. *Jackie, 10* • I wish I could meet my whole family and they all could get along and I could be a teacher and a famous basketball player and my family could be rich and by clothes. *Edward, 9* • I wish that I can live with my dad forever. *Vicki, 7* • I wish I had a nice pretty garden. *Briana, 8* • I wish I can always make my mom proud of me. I wish I can go to college and get a bigger education. *Vanessa, 13* • I wish I had a mansion so I could help poor people who don't have a place to stay. *Antonio, 9* • I wish I could see my dad. I wish my mom would have a happy life. I wish I could go to college and get a job so I can take care of my family. *Linda, 7* • I wish I can stay here in the kids cafe. *Jasmine, 6* • I wish I can stay in one house. *Anthony, 7* • I wish people would stop doing drugs. I wish the law would only let policemen and women use guns. I wish there was no such thing as rapists in the world. *Rhonda, 13* • I wish the mayor would help the poor people and fix the earth. Age 11 • I wish I could be a artist now. *Allie, 7* • I wish I could have known Sister Gus. *Jordan, 9* • I wish I can end all fighting and violence to the world and make it a better place. *Eva, 9* • I wish the world was nice. I wish my dad would take me to the zoo. *Dejah, 6* • I wish I could work at KFC when I get big. *Maritza, 6* • I wish I can stay at Kids Cafe forever. I wish Marget and Jery and Sister Sallie and Sister Di was younger so they can live longer. *Eva, 9* • I wish I would go to college and get a good education and get a diploma and get a scholarship and when I grow up I am going to be a pediatrician for breathing treatments. *Chantelle, 11* • I wish I could move into a better neighborhood where people would be nicer. *Roshina, 11* • I wish everyone could get along with each other. *Alison, 8* • I wish people would stop being violent. I wish that people would not influence others with drugs. *Roshina, 11* • I wish there were more volunteers here. *Krystin* • I wish that I can stay with my dad. *Anthony, 7* • I wish that Sister Gus could come back to the kids cafe. *Jordan, 9* • I wish for my sister to come back home. *Kristina, 9* • I wish we never had school. I wish the world would change in a good way. I wish I had a better life. I wish there was no fighting ever. I wish there was no killing. *Shana, 11* • I wish I can have long hair. I wish I can see my dad. *Linda, 7* • I wish the robbers would stop and people would stop polluting and fighting and doing stupid stuff and going to jail. I wish people would stop doing drugs because all your doing is killing yourself. *Tamika, 11* • I wish the world could become a better place because people are becoming woster and woster. • I wish my family would get along. I wish I could be gymnastic and a teacher. *Rikki, 12* • I wish that when I grow up I can be a singer. *Jordan, 9* • I wish that I could move and get new stuff. *Kimberly, 9* • I wish I could be a mom when I grow up. I wish I could move to a bigger house in a better neighborhood. *Maritza, 6* • I wish my aunt B would get better. *Manny, 7* • I wish I could go to a better school. *Tobeth, 9* • I wish when I get older I can play in the national hockey league. *Brian, 12* • I wish my mom has a happy marriage. I wish I can go to college and get a basketball degree. *Kiara, 11* • I wish that Jery would give me 25 kids cafe money. *Jordan, 9* • I wish I have lots of money. *Tyler* • I wish I was so famous. I wish that Sister Gus was back from heaven so that people could be good. *Meghan, 9* • I wish I can have more freedom. I wish I can be a better person. *Amenda, 12* • I wish Sister Gus was here so I could play with her. *Jasmine, 8* • I wish Sister Gus was stel alive so she would know me. *Cheyenne, 9* • I wish I would go to school until I graduate. *Jose, 10* • I wish that Sister Gus was at Kids Cafe today. *Krystin, 9* • I wish I could be a basketball player, a soccer player, and a fireman. James 6 • I wish I could be the mayor of Erie and give schools more money so they could build better schools. *Roman, 10* • I wish that I can get A's and B's in school so I can get a better job when I grow up. *Labraya, 9* • I wish I could be good so I don't get in so much trouble. Peter • I wish nobody would fight. *Ronnie, 12* • I wish everyone would tell the truth. *Clifton, 9* • I wish that everybody would be nice. I wish everyone would help one another. I wish everyone would share. *Quayvon, 8* • I wish people at school were nicer to me. *Joseph, 9* • I wish that I could donate money and food to the poor. *Marissa, 10* • I wish the world would change by respecting others. *Teada, 11* • I wish that I was old enough to have my own car. *Lizamanelle, 12*

When You Fish Upon a Star

artists: Conrad Kraus and Kids Cafe

patrons: In Loving Memory of Pamela Jane's Grandparents, Finish Thompson, Inc., Modern Industries, Inc., & Fr. Thomas Dugan

location: East 10th & Parade Streets

Inspirational Award

A heartening catch

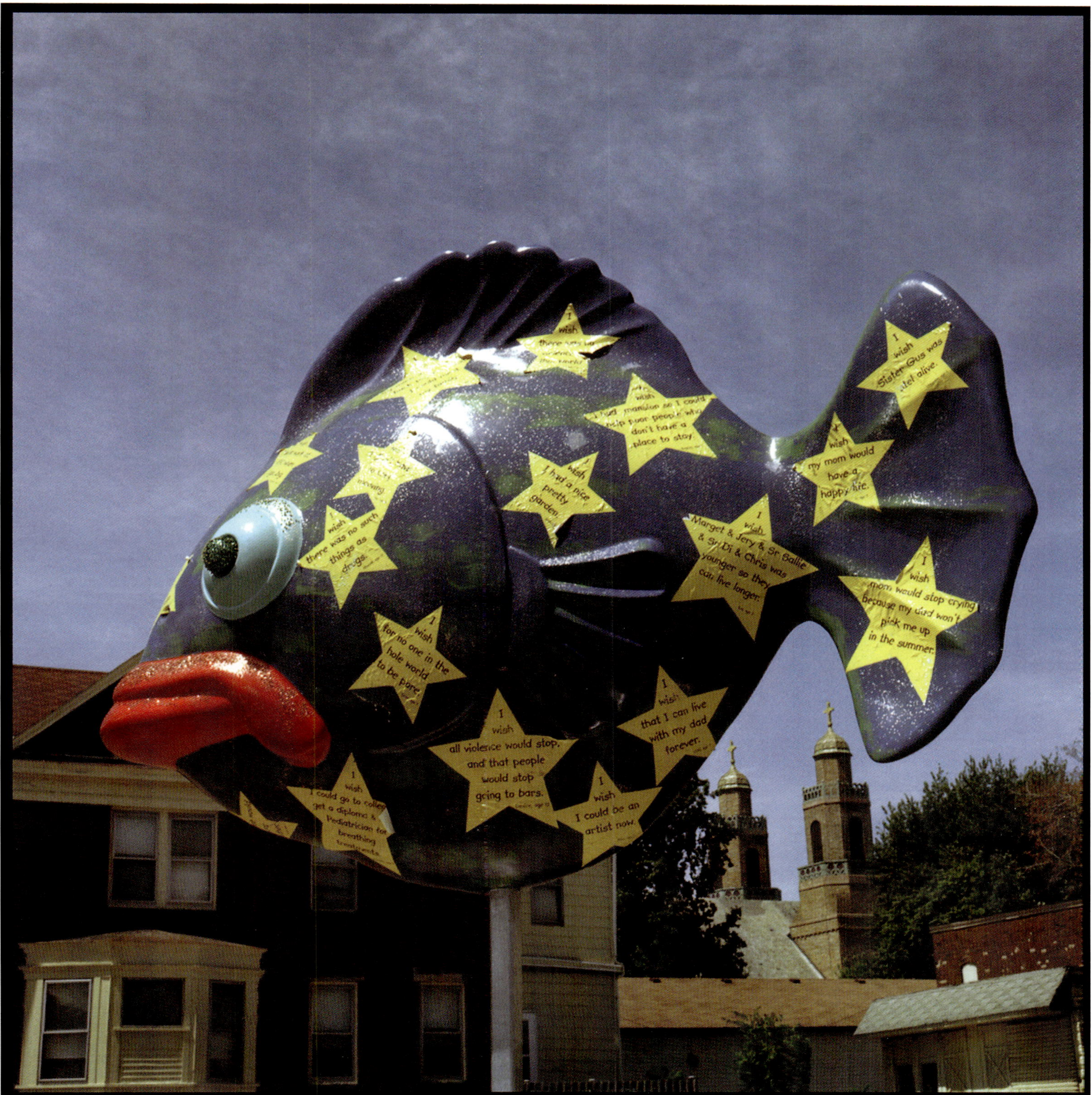
I wish Sister Gus was
alive.
I wish I had mansion so I could help poor people who don't have a place to stay.
I wish my mom would have a happy life.
I wish I had a nice pretty garden.
I wish there was no such things as drugs.
I wish Marget & Jery & Sr Sallie & Sr Di & Chris was younger so they can live longer.
I wish mom would stop crying because my dad won't pick me up in the summer.
I wish for no one in the hole world to be pore.
I wish that I can live with my dad forever.
I wish all violence would stop, and that people would stop going to bars.
I wish I could be an artist now.
I wish I could go to college get a diploma & Pediatrician for breathing

“The most beautiful woman I’ve ever met”

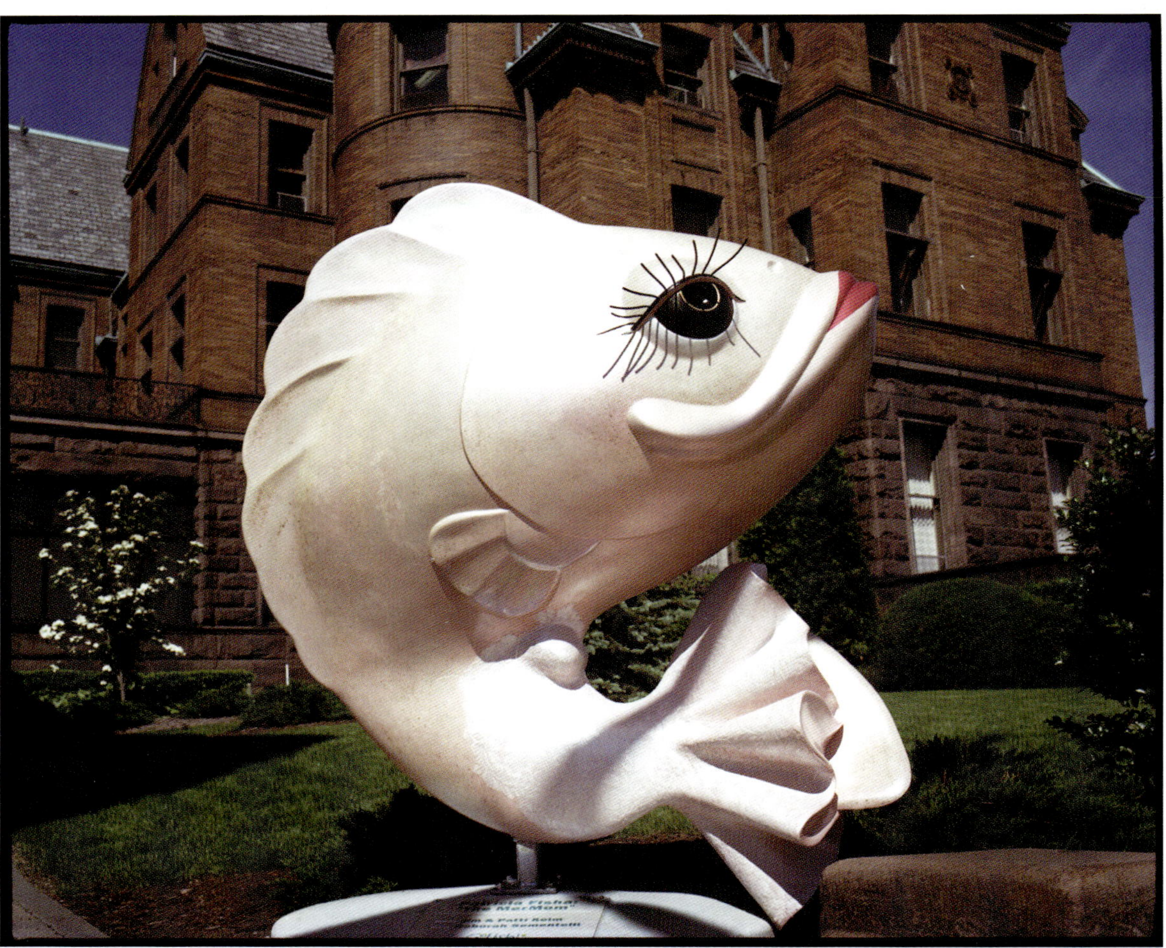

Patricia Fisha: The “MerMom”
artist: Deborah Sementelli
patrons: Jim & Patty Keim
location: Peach Street & South Park Row

Child’s Play Award
Full of color and fun for little ones

That’s how Jim Keim described his mother to Debbie Sementelli, whose challenge was to capture Patricia Keim’s essence in fiberglass form. She was also portrayed as bold, progressive, and even having a movie-star quality. Before beginning to envision the fish’s design, the artist met Pat at a breakfast, and was struck with this thought: *she is the epitome of a lady.* So Debbie dove into the project, aiming to create a very attractive, ageless, classic-looking female creature. It is, in final form, the opposite of a mermaid— rather, a fish turning into a beautiful woman— or a “MerMom.”

Patricia Fisha looks particularly stunning in the evening, when the night light brings out the iridescence of the paint that costumes her eyelids and her back. Pat Keim, on the other hand, is lovely at any time of the day.

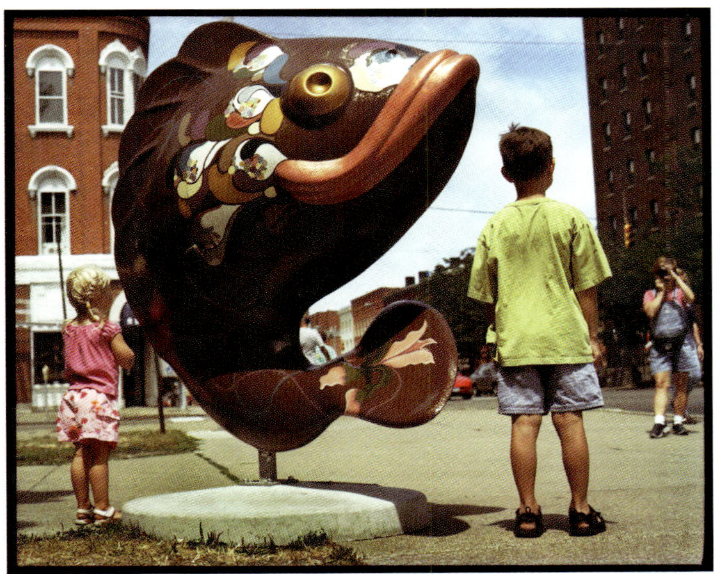

Le Poisson
artist: Heather Riehl
patrons: Tom Rivon, Alisun Kovach, Grandma Barbara, The Colony Plaza, Walnut Creek Grill, & John & Susan Moore
location: Perry Square, State Street & North Park Row

"There are so many people who I see taking photos of the fish, taking photos with the fish, or just studying them. This project brought pride back to the Erie community– it really shows how much talent we have here in the city."

Lisa Manendo

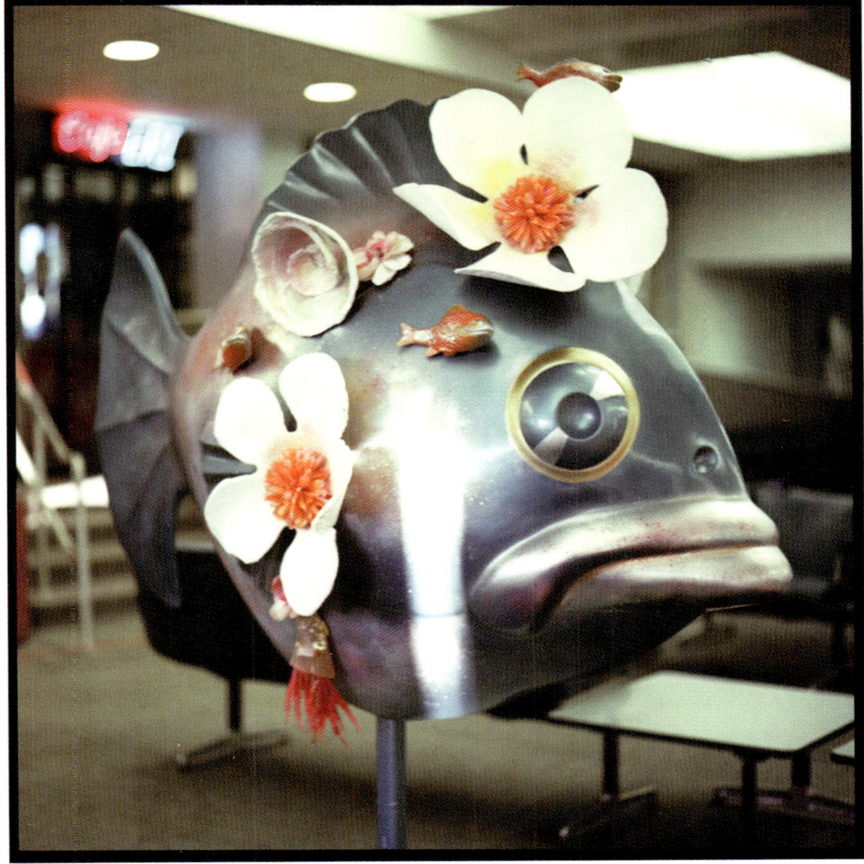

"Sweet Leilonie," Heavenly Flower
artist: Matta D.
patron: Coldwell Banker Select, Realtors
location: Erie International Airport

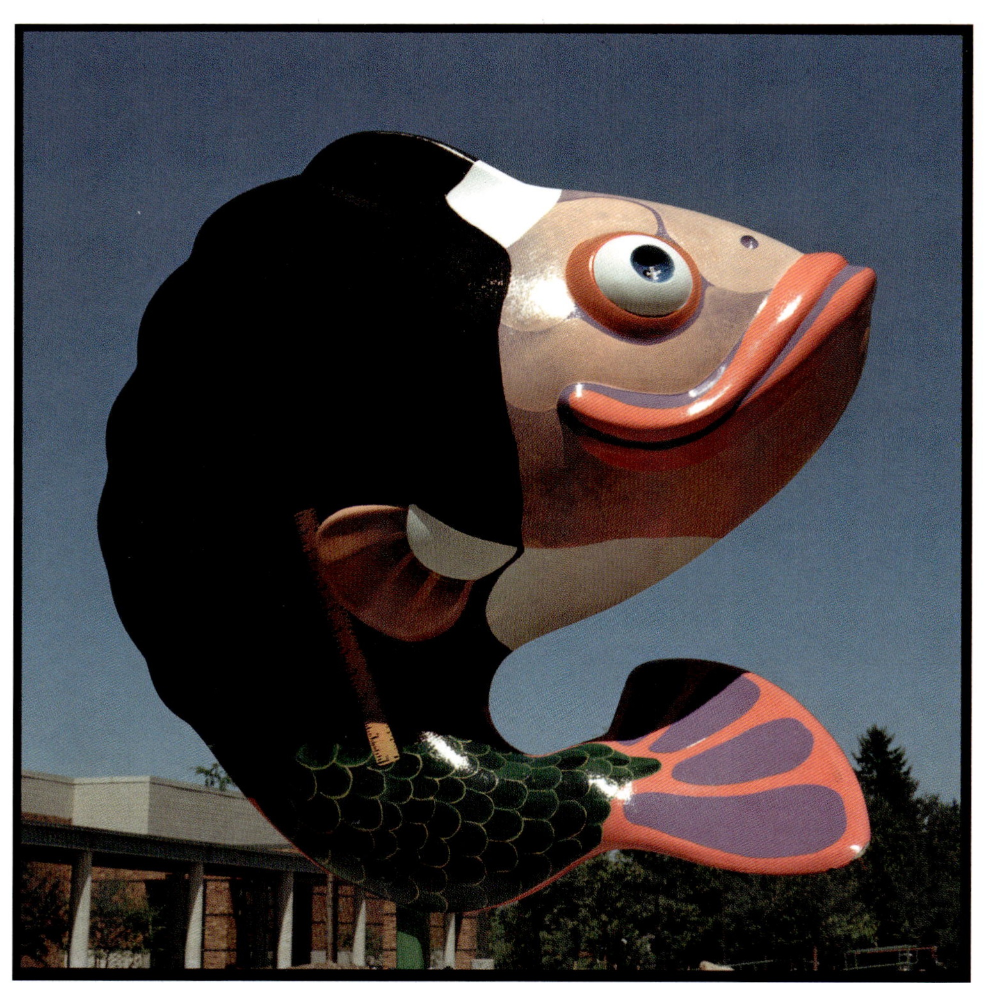

Sr. Carpe Diem, Fishter of Mercy
artist: Jamie Borowicz
patron: James & Mary Ann Baldauf for Mercyhurst Preparatory School
location: 538 East Grandview Boulevard

ahabitualartist

Jamie Borowicz, an art teacher at Mercyhurst Prep, works with the Sisters of Mercy, and knows plenty of nuns. And when he decided to create his fish in a sisterly sort of spirit, "nobody said a heck of a lot."

His muse for Sister Carpe Diem, Fishter of Mercy, was Sister Bertha— an archetypal nun who taught Latin at Mercyhurst until she was 90 years old. The last wimple-wearing woman at the school, Sister Bertha wore a full habit to the floor and a rosary around her waist. She was a sharp-minded lady who ran the bookstore and retired just five years ago. Jamie enjoyed joking around with her, playing word games and visiting.

He found her to be a wonderful woman, and she truly was the inspiration for this GoFish! work of art.

sheworeanitsybitsyteeny weeny...

According to the artist, who estimates Sadie's brassiere size to be at least a DD, "Putting boobs on fish is not easy." Her bikini was originally to be leopard, but then he decided to make it polka-dotted (the dots alone took 3.5 hours to paint). While Michael's mother badgered him to create Erin Brockofish, he instead was determined to create Sexy Sadie, inspired by the Beatles song of the same name.

Michael Nathan, Sexy Sadie's creator, was kind enough to supply the Fish Commish with her resume:

Name: Sexy Sadie GoFish!
Occupation: swimsuit model
Sign: Pisces
Favorite foods: chocolate bourbon, truffles, shrimp, guppies
Favorite book: Moby Dick
Favorite band: Hot Tuna, Phish
Favorite movie: 2000 Leagues Under the Sea
Hobbies: water ballet, scuba diving

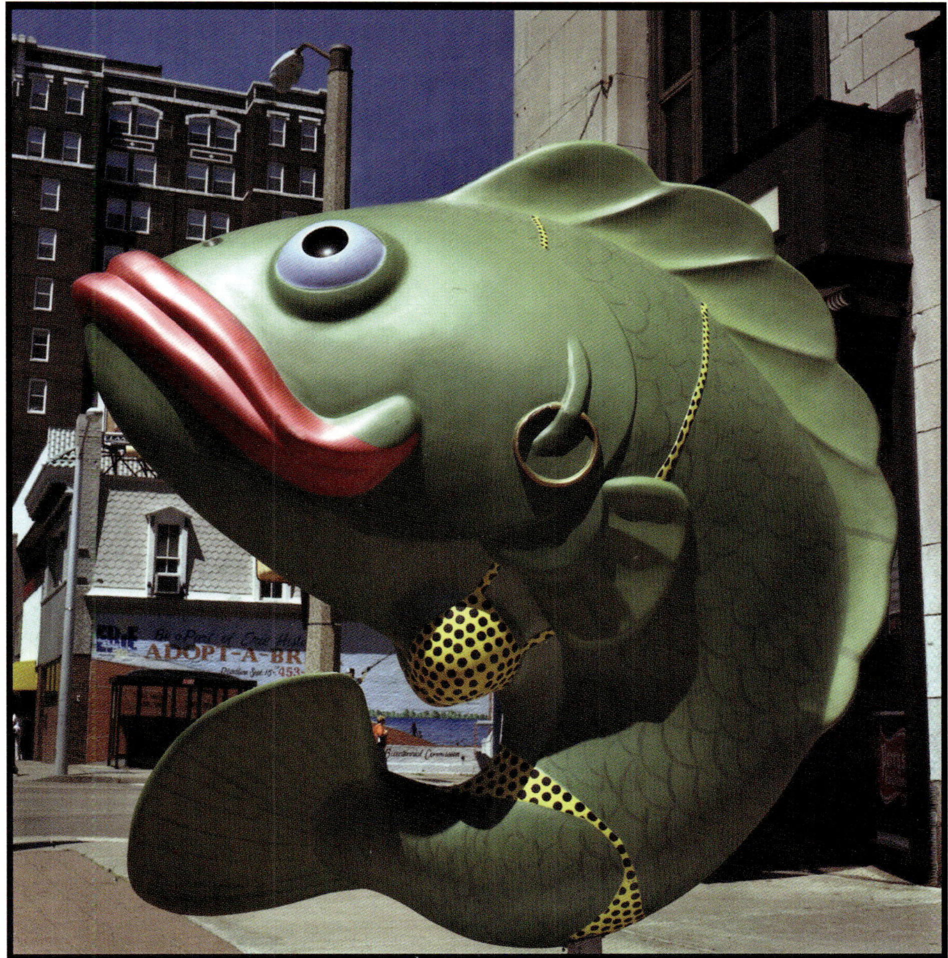

Sexy Sadie
artist: Michael Nathan
patron: In memory of Tom Gay by Joy Gay
location: 10th & State Streets

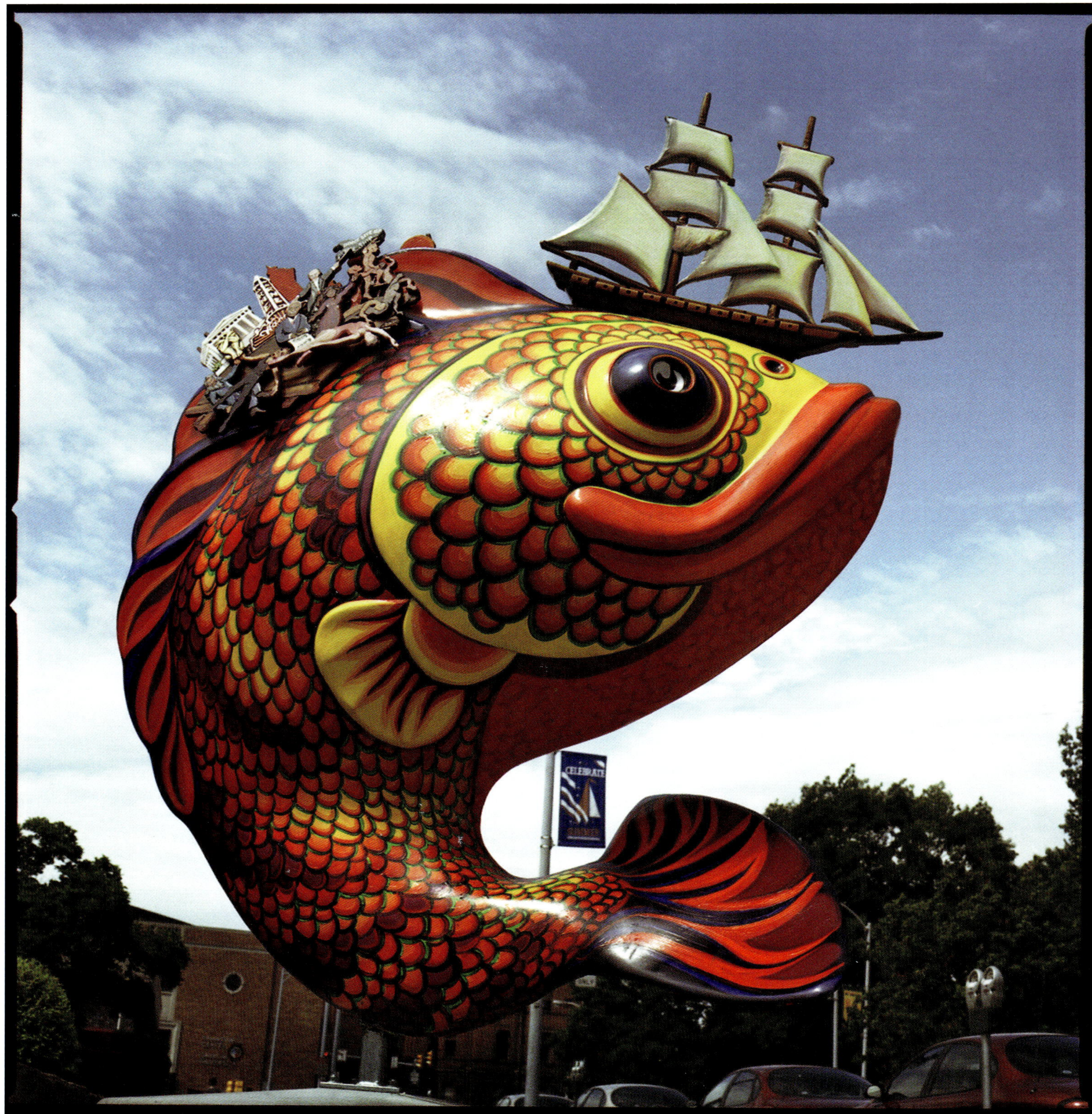
CELEBRATE

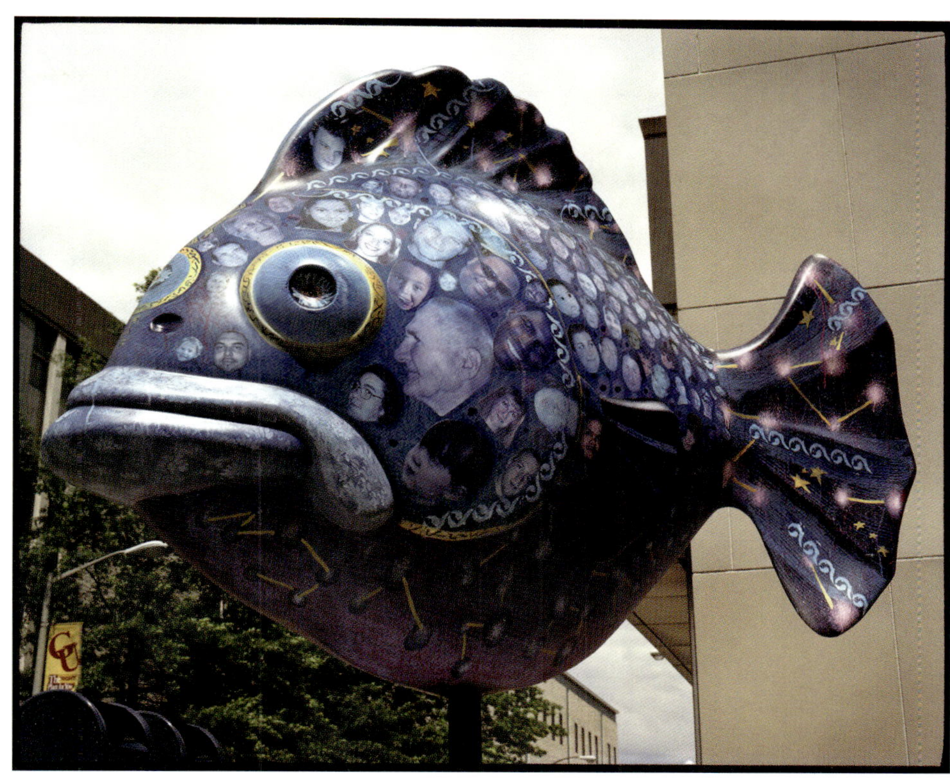

Rolly Polly Fishheads
artist: Kris Risto
patron: donated to the Greater Erie Community Action Committee by the Greater Erie Economic Development Corporation
location: West 9th & Peach Streets

recipeforlakeerieperch

created by Chef Matthew V. Sarbak, C.W.C.
of Matthew's Trattoria:

Lake Erie Perch is so tasty indeed
That is why I wrote this recipe, you see.
To catch this wiley and tasty fishee,
You need luck and patience to the tenth degree.
A chubby nightcrawler is always of help.
One must be both nimble and quick to pull this stunt off.
I prefer to skin, bone and dip my little perchie,
In milk, flour and breadcrumbs so she's dressed to the tee.
A hot cast iron skillet, I'd say, is an essential need,
A splash of olive oil, and now we're ready to proceed.
Golden brown on both sides, a touch of lemon and lime,
I tell you the truth, it's very sublime.
A dollop of butter, and crack of the peppermill,
Now all I can say is BON APPETITO!

Erie Perch
artist: Carole Werder
patron: City of Erie
location: State Street & South Park Row

Erie Award
Best represents the City of Erie

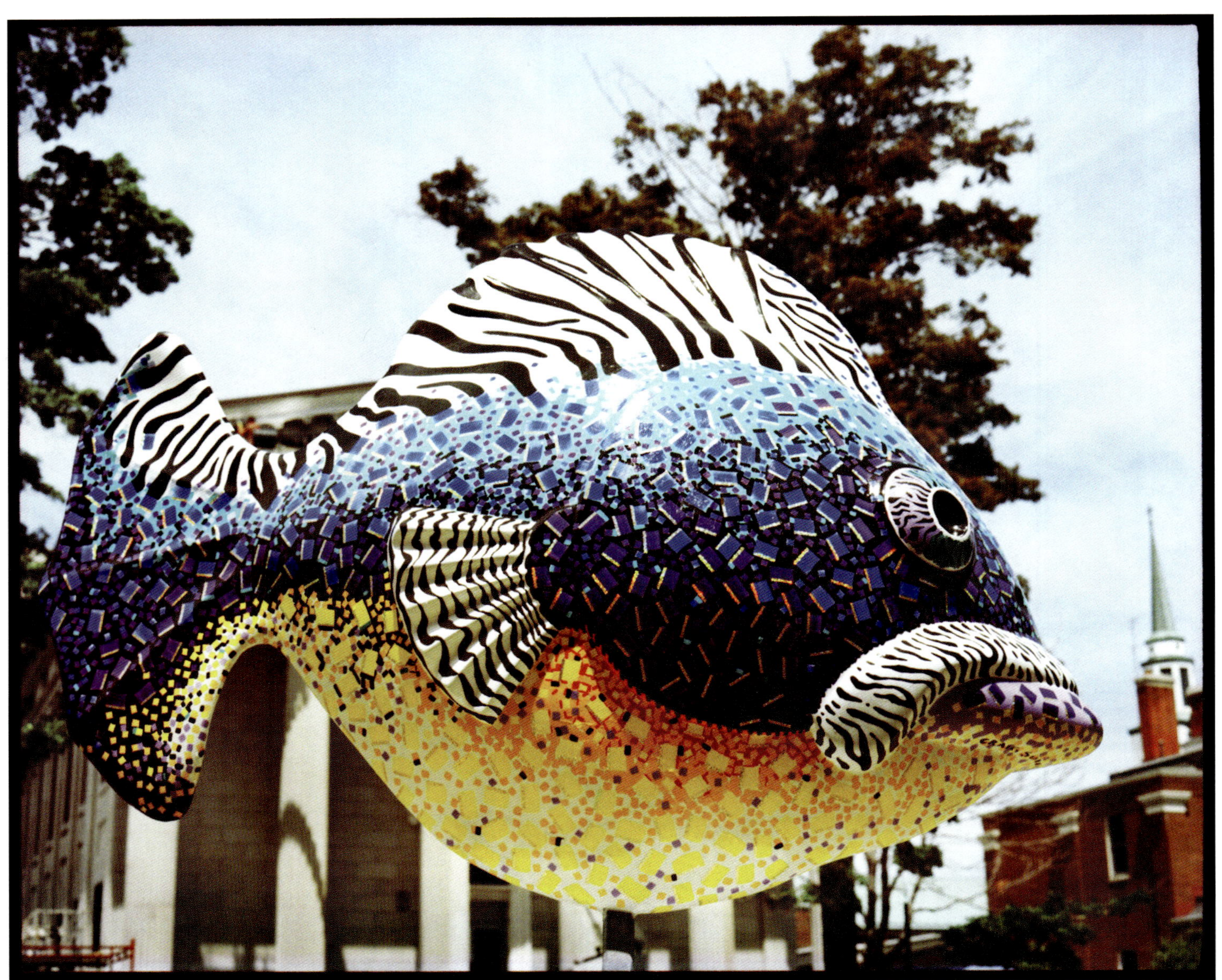

The Philan"tropic" Fish
artist: Craig Sundberg
patron: Erie Community Foundation
location: 127 West 6th Street

"Thanks to all of those who worked so hard to create this exhibit. As someone who has been to Erie many times over the past 40 years, I can honestly say that this exhibit was the best thing I have ever seen."

Michael Bruno

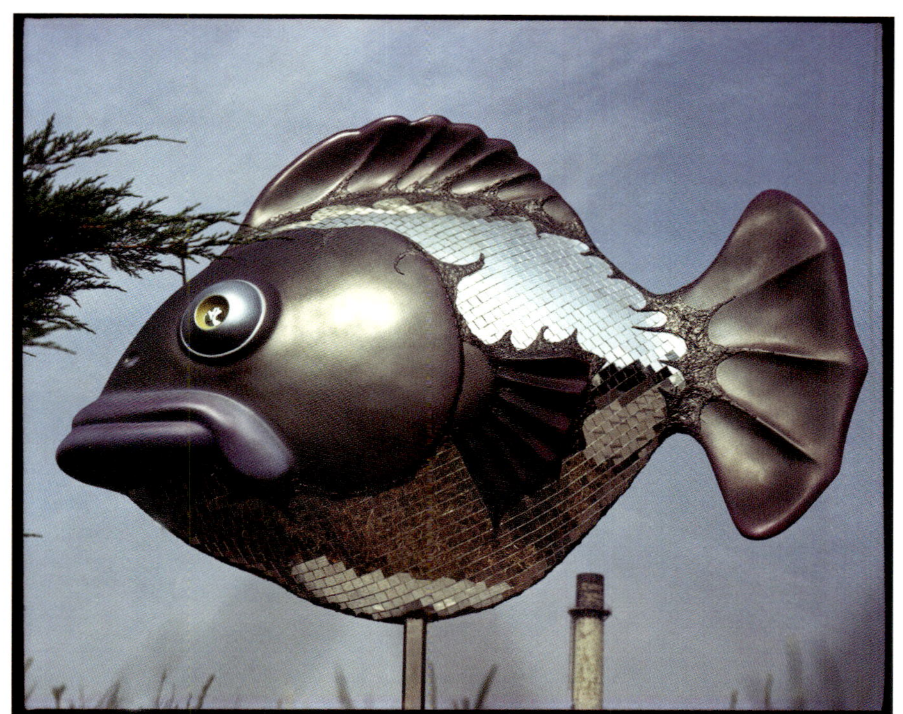

Reflecto-fish
artist: David Collins
patron: Richard Morrison Foundation
location: Dobbins Landing

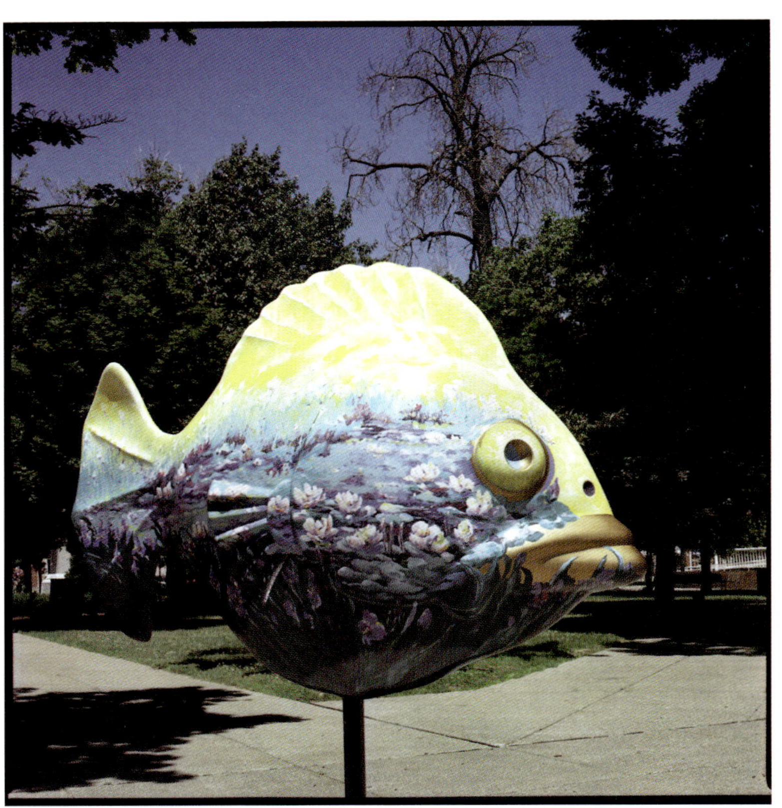

Peaceful Journey through Giverny
artist: Joyce Perowicz
patron: Dusckas Funeral Home
location: Perry Square, Peach Street & South Park Row

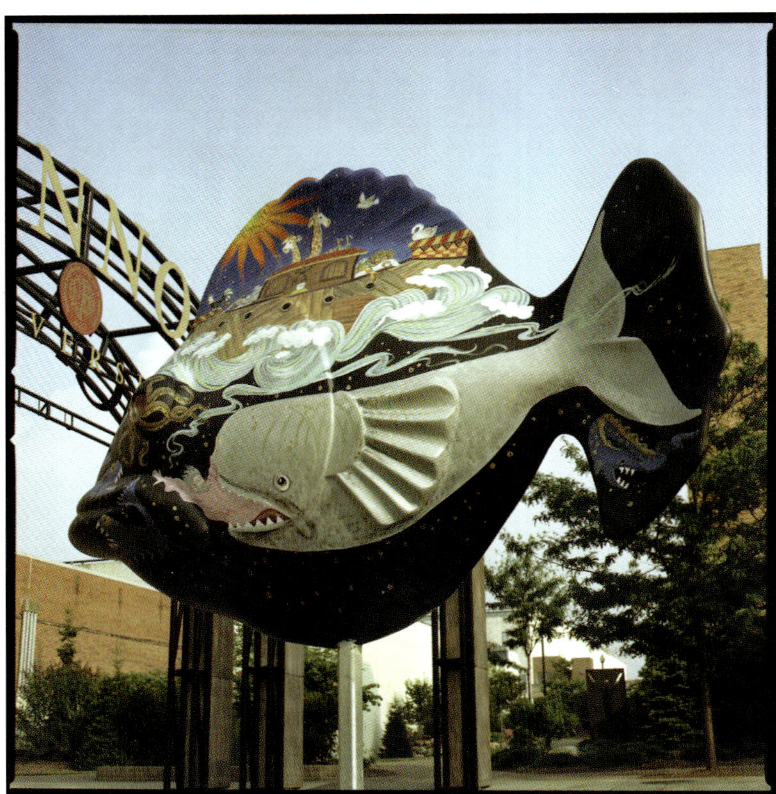

Yesterday and Today
artist: Susan Black
patron: The Schulze Family
location: 124 West 7th Street

fish-eyeview

Joey Grego gets a fish's-eye view. From behind the window of Studio Three Down Town, his business located at 8th and Peach, he sees hundreds of people, out and about, every day. They are individuals and they are families, they are young and they are very old. And what they have in common is this: they all have GoFish! maps tucked in their back pockets.

But Joey's not surprised by the enthusiasm Erie's shown for the project—he experienced it firsthand with Fishing Ships, a whimsical work of art designed to appeal to adults and children alike. As the fish would be located down near the water, he used colors that would blend in with the boats, the dock, and the entire area. And then, when the fish was being installed, he painted the base to match the fish, right then and there.

And the people were drawn to it. Folks from all walks of life, ones who live right in the neighborhood as well as those who drove up and parked, gathered round to watch. It took Joey 1.5 hours to finish painting the base, but the 25 or so people who came together that day didn't care—they stayed the entire time, supporting him until the fish was complete.

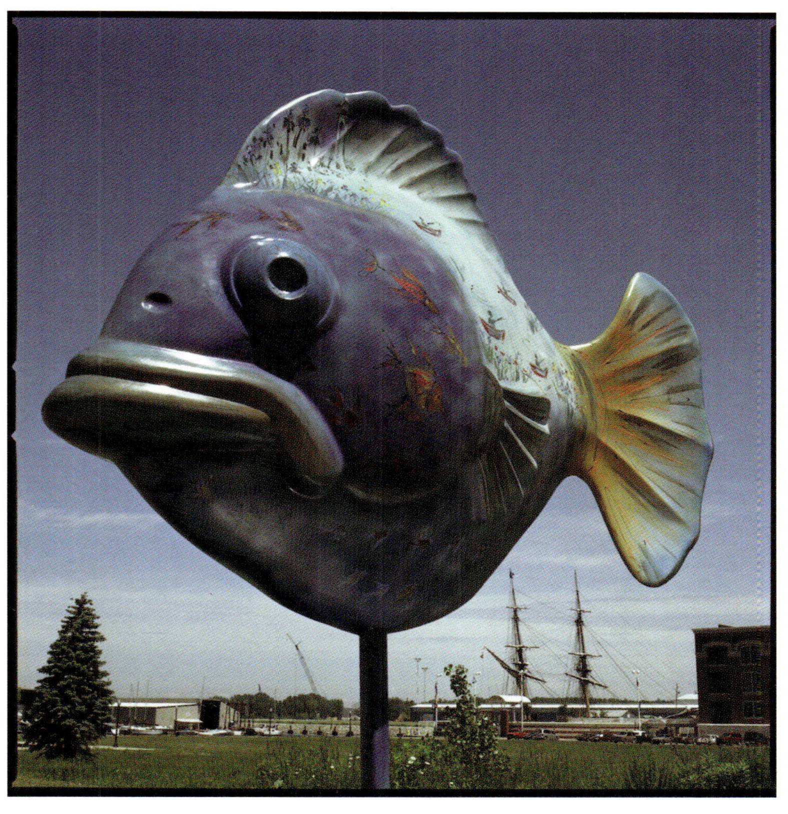

Fishing Ships
artist: Joey Grego
patrons: Diane & David Blake
location: East Front & State Streets

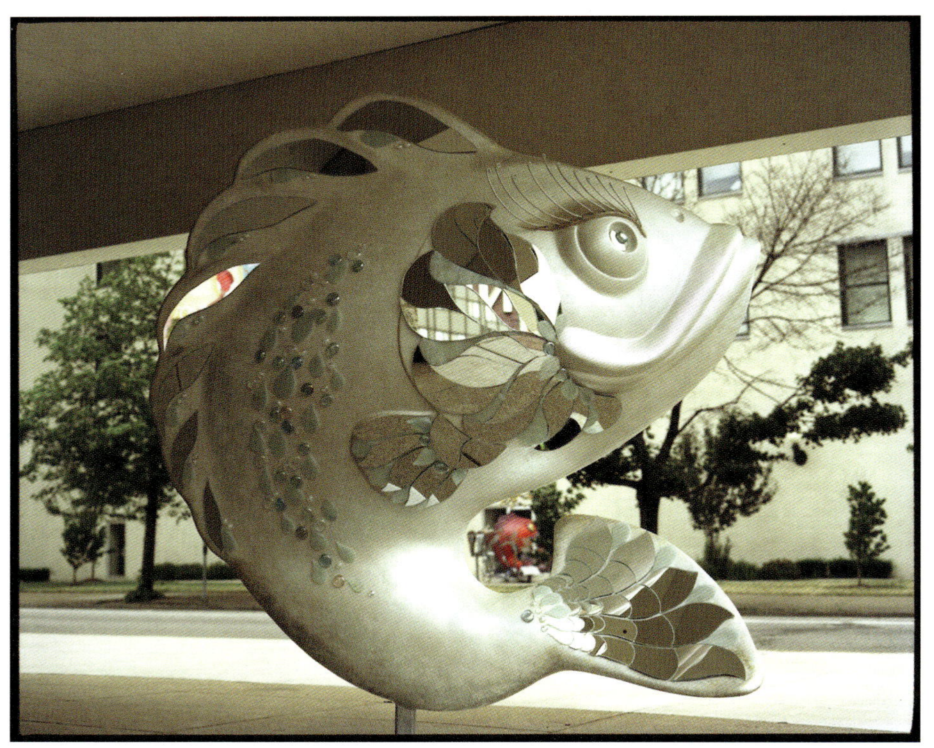

Blissful Reflections
artist: Cathy MacGregor
patron: Robert & Christie Ferrier
location: 8th & State Streets

Photogenic Award
An attractive catch

ametalforeffort

"He calls it his fish; I call it my fish." But there is no custody battle here: D.W. Martin enthuses about how well he and sponsor Howard Lincoln worked together in creating Recycle for the Halibut.

It began with the idea of fly fishing. Which turned into a flying fish. Then D.W. started thinking about airplanes, wings, and propellers. He created a model from Styrofoam and aluminum cans, and brought it to Howard. And they agreed to go ahead with it, albeit with a few alterations that would make it look more like a sea plane with pontoons, like an airplane fuselage all pop-riveted together.

In the spirit of his sponsor's business, D.W. fashioned the eyes, lips, propellers, hubs, some of the trim, and the pontoon shapes from recycled sheet metal, all supplied by Howard. Being a sculptor, the artist wanted to manipulate the form a bit, understanding that the fish still needed to be present in the image. His goal was to make it more sculptural, different, humorous and eye-catching.

In the early stages of the process, D.W. appreciated the creative license Howard allowed him. Then, about halfway through, Howard began to better see D.W.'s vision and got excited. Howard's eyes lit up and he said, "This is really going to work."

Recycle for the Halibut
artist: D.W. Martin
patron: Lincoln Metals
location: Dobbins Landing

Traffic Stopper Award
So alluring, it brings passers-by to a halt

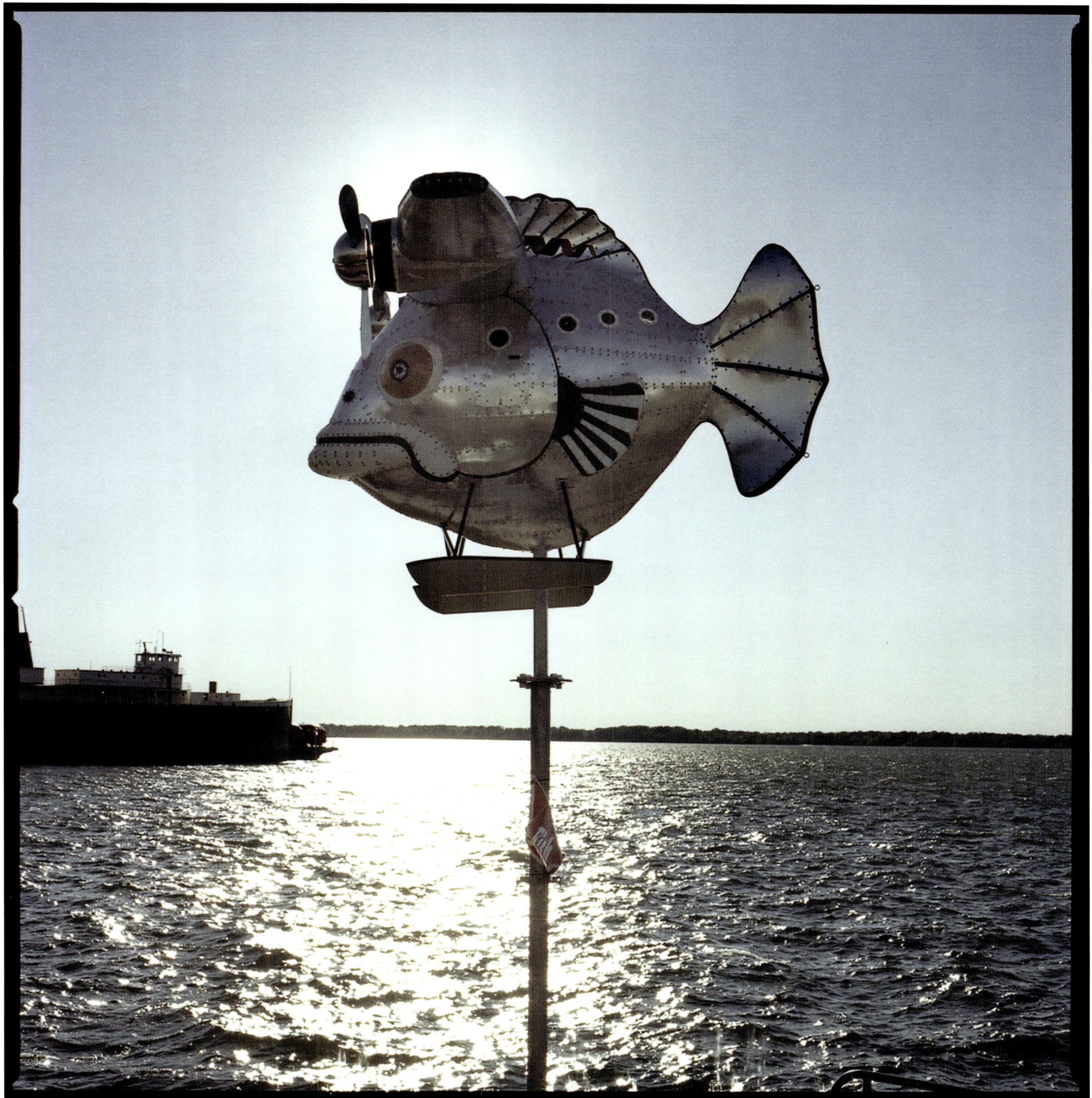

"It has taken us over a month, but we now have photos of all the fish. Traveling in and around Erie this summer has been so much fun, and we have met so many nice people....We now know all the streets–even which ones are one way!"

Carlene & Bob Stroup

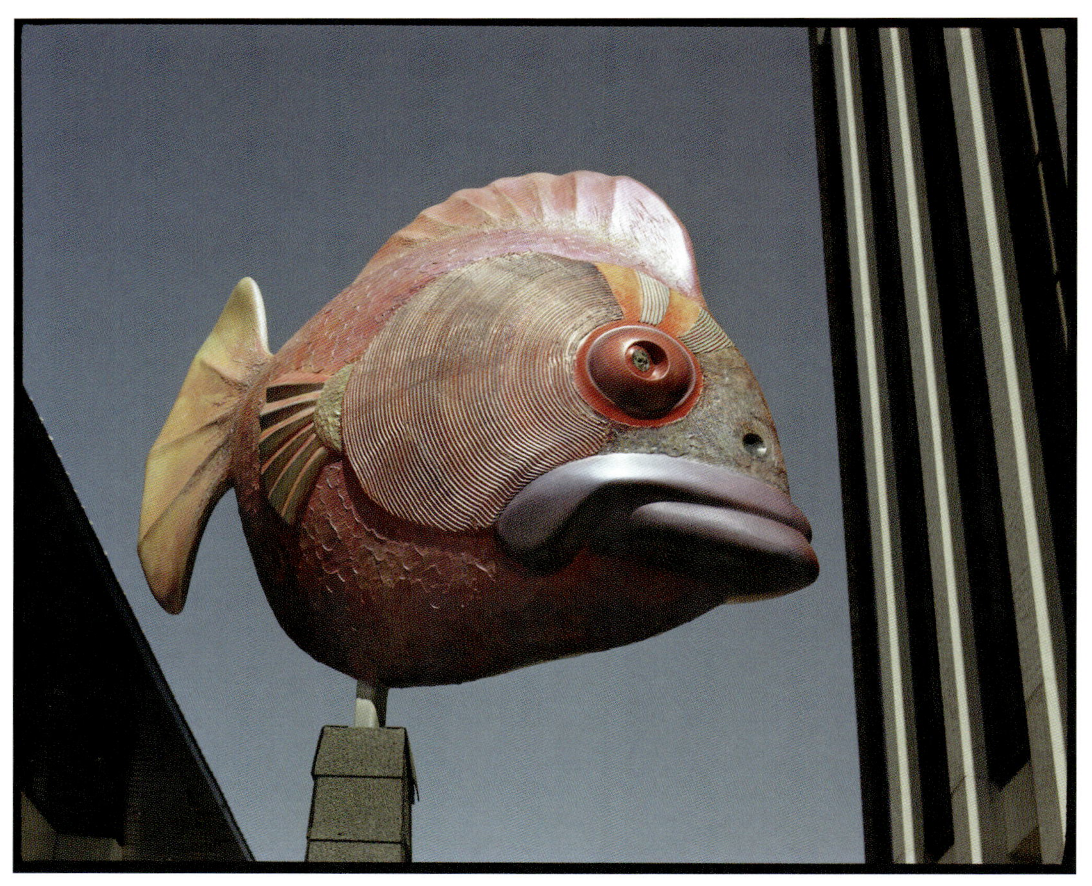

One Fish, Two Fish, Red Fish, Blue Fish
artist: John Vahanian
patron: First National Bank
location: 711 State Street

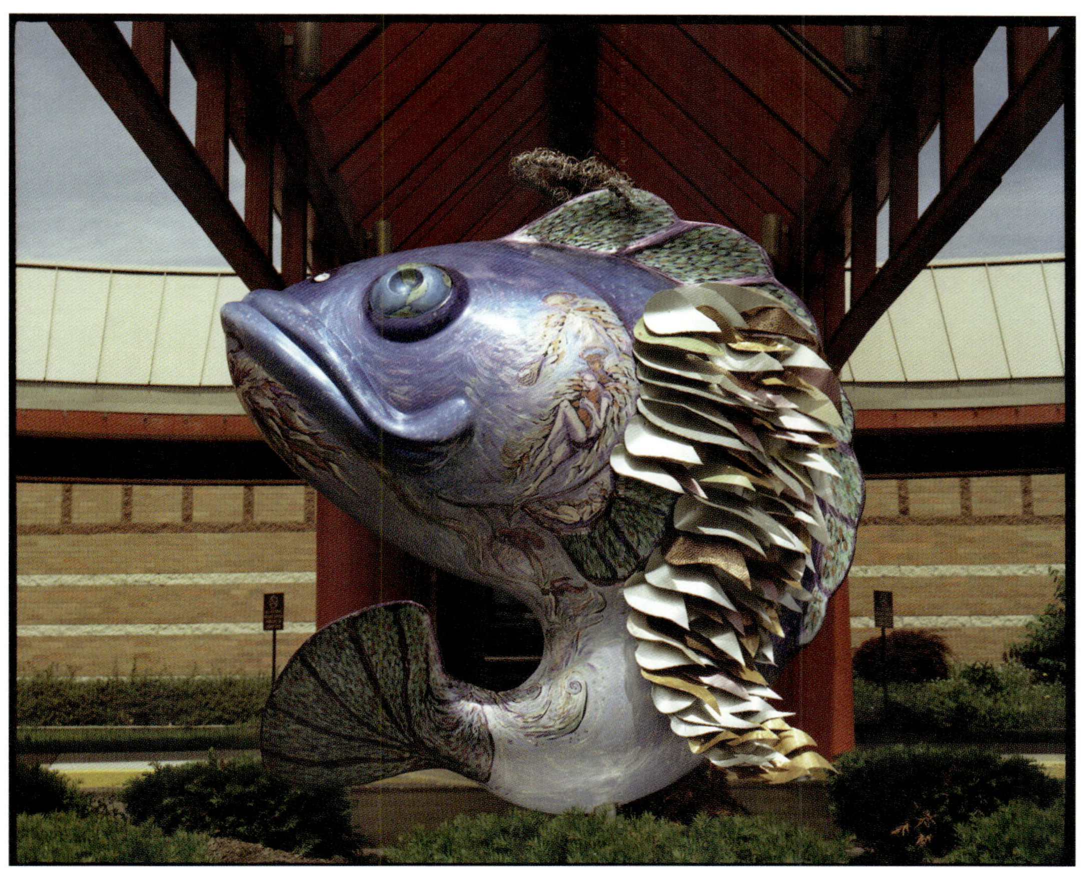

ālo
artist: Heather Hertel
patron: Schaffner, Knight, Minnaugh & Co., P.C.
location: 2500 West 12th Street
Inspirational Award
A heartening catch

letyourfish beyourguide

When Heather Hertel heard about the GoFish! project from her brother, she desperately wanted to get involved. Heather's boss at the Erie Club even allowed her to make inquiries to members in her attempt to get matched up with a patron. So, when project advisor Susan Black-Keim came in for dinner one night, Heather didn't hesitate to march up and hand her a copy of her resume, saying "I'll do anything to get a fish."

As it turned out, Susan had a meeting scheduled with Jim Schaffner the next day, and he agreed to sponsor her fish. Heather got the good news on Valentine's Day, when Susan came into the restaurant to tell her in person.

Heather's fish was created in memory of her mother, Michele, who was a cancer survivor for a full decade. Since the fish would be located at the Regional Cancer Center, watching over the people walking in and out of the facility each day, she decided to design an angel fish. In reading all about angels in different cultures, she found that alo, which means "spiritual guide" in Hopi Indian language, is a healer.

"My mom is now one of the healers, watching over us," Heather said. "I hope these wings carry you when you need a little lift."

ready,set,gofish!

It took less than five minutes for this match to be made.

Last winter, back when the lake was still frozen, Susie McAllister ran into longtime friends Bruce and Nancy Kern at (of all places!) the Yacht Club. Someone brought up the subject of fish. None of them knew the timeline, the details, or even the cost.

Bruce said, "If you'll be our artist, we'll be your sponsor." Susie said, "If you'll be my sponsor, I'd love to be your artist."

And the rest is fishistory.

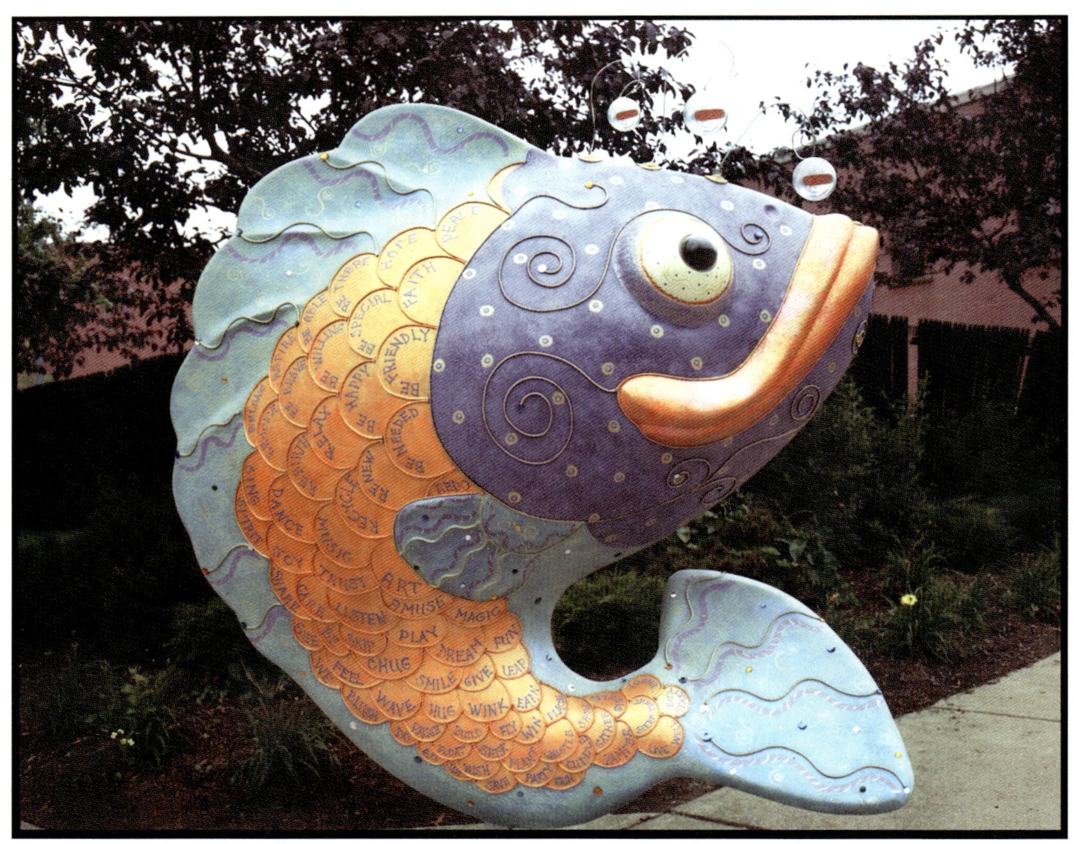

Food for Thought
artist: Susie McAllister
patron: C.A. Curtze Company
location: East 5th & French Streets

"My grandmother is so happy to see so many people downtown again, like when she was a little girl. Such a simple idea done so well, gives everyone an opportunity to say "hello" to others in the community."

Maura Detter

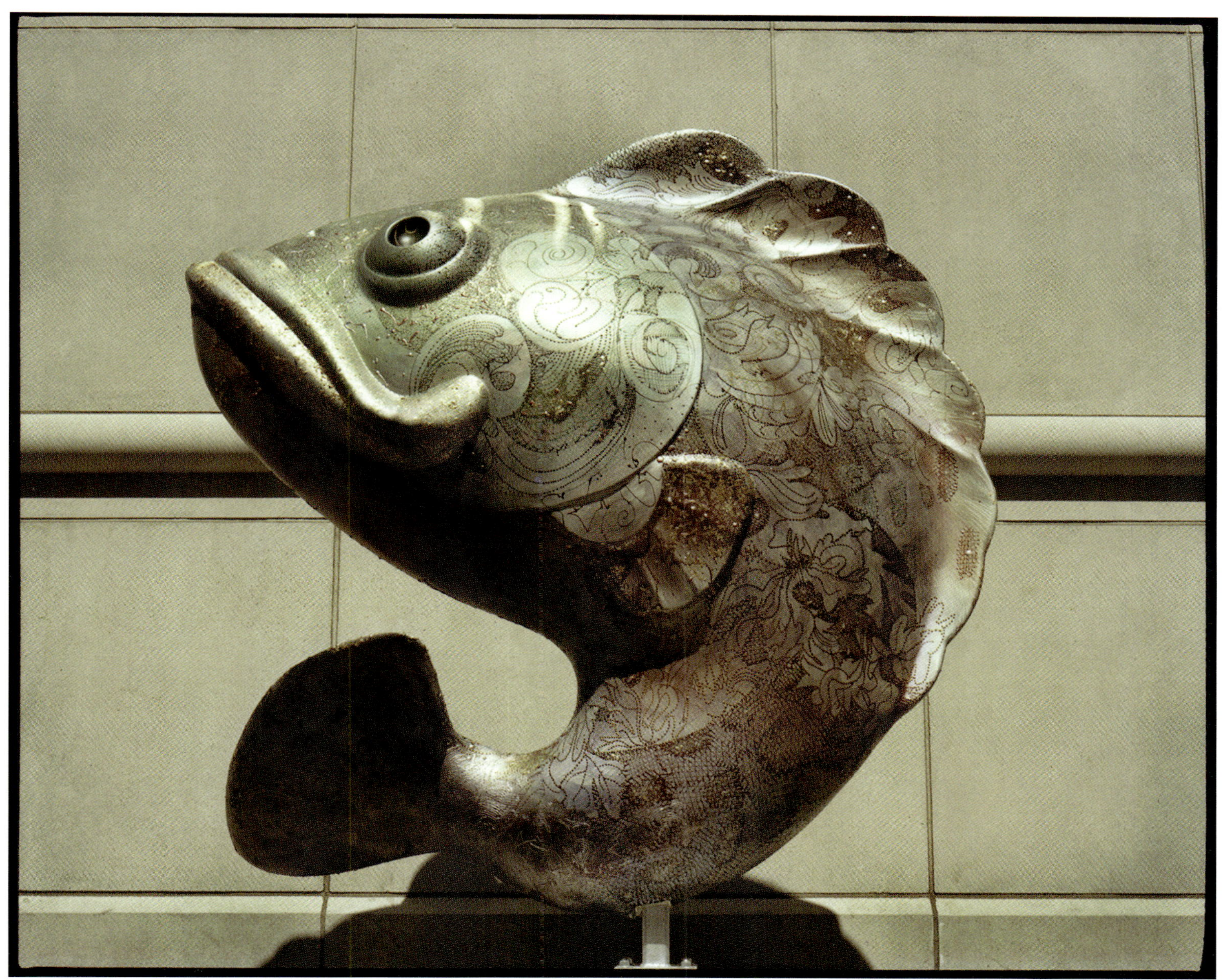

Stocks & Ponds
artist: Susan Kemenyffy
patron: PNC Financial Services Group/Hilliard Lyons
location: 9th & State Streets

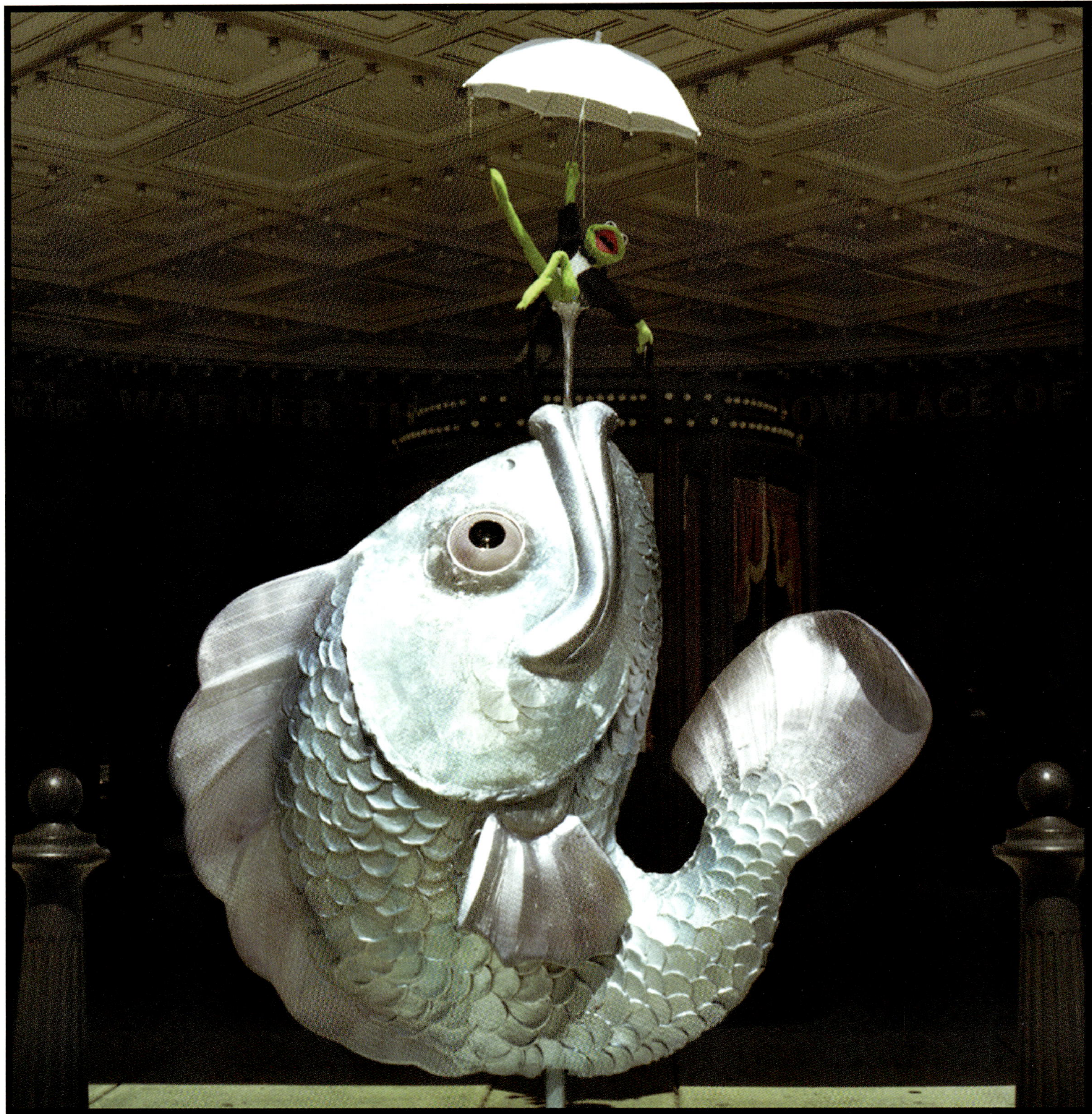

Swingin' in the Rain
artist: David L. Seitzinger
patron: The Kada Gallery
location: 811 State Street

Smiley Face Award
Brings an immediate smile

Charlie, in Honor of Charlie Scalise
artist: Abigail Brace
patron: St. Joseph's Apartments & HANDS
location: 517 Maryland Avenue

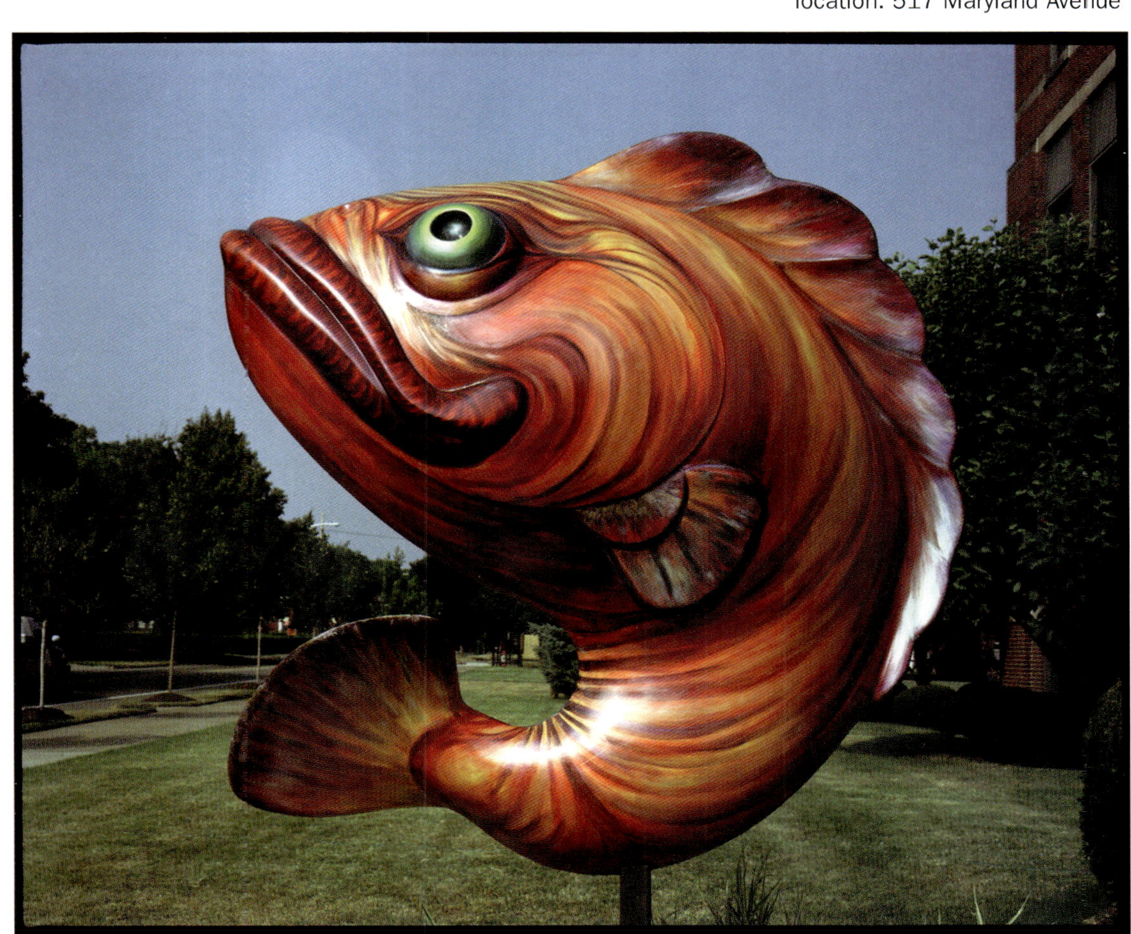

mynameischarlie.

Charlie Scalise was on the board of HANDS (Housing and Neighborhood Development Service) since its inception in 1965. He was its executive director for more than 20 years.

You might not have known he was the executive director, though— he could have been anyone. Spending very little time behind a desk, making a effort to stop by St. Joseph's and the other buildings every day, chatting with the tenants and staff, making a point to introduce himself to people he didn't know and learning about who they were, working shoulder-to-shoulder with the employees, observing, fixing things that needed to be fixed, quietly, magically, making things better...he could have been anyone.

But to the residents of St. Joseph's, he was *someone*. And when the entire building had the chance to vote on what to call the fish that would be a permanent piece of art on the front lawn for many years to come, the decision was made by an overwhelming majority: they would call it Charlie.

notthethinone,notthefatone

The hair took the longest to make.

Bill Figurski's Elvis-inspired fish, Elfish Presley, is not a satire but a tribute. Symbolic of the heyday of Elvis Presley's career. The era of the big-collared shirt, the signature glasses, the pompadour hair.

While no Elvis, Bill himself was a musician for many years, playing keyboard and sax for pop, rock and jazz bands. His high regard for Elvis' rags-to-riches story inspired the fish, and he even rigged it so Elvis' songs play nonstop through an outdoor speaker system wired to a CD player located inside the hospital.

Bill has been approached by Elvis fans many times near the fish—even one in the international Elvis fan club! But the most memorable visitor was an actual Elvis impersonator—complete with lime-green large-lapeled shirt, chrome glasses and big hair—getting his photo taken with the fish.

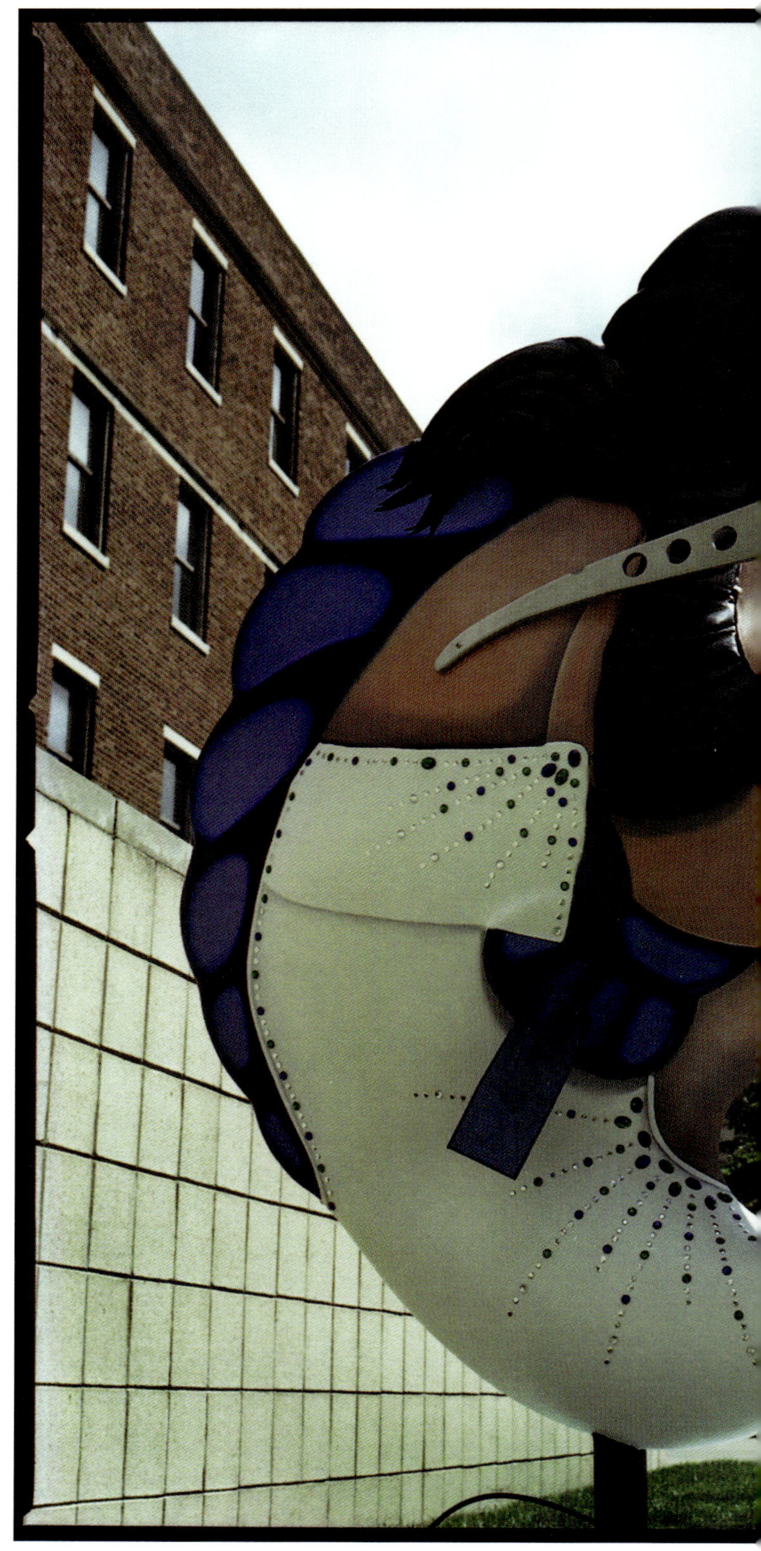

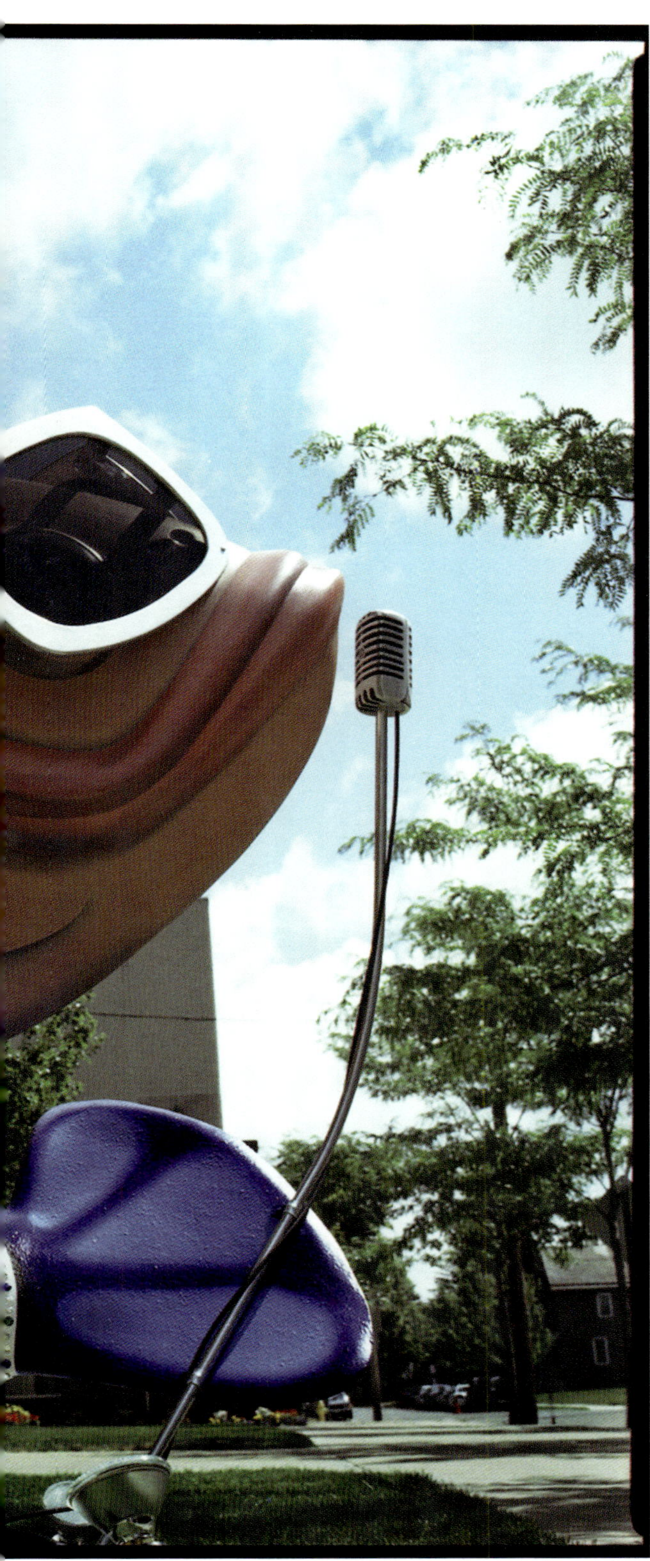

"In early July, "The King of Rock and Roll" arrived at Saint Vincent. Not Elvis Presley, but Elfish Presley, complete with slicked back jet black hair, a rhinestone studded jump suit, cool sunglasses and microphone. What makes Elfish extra-special to the Saint Vincent community of caregivers is the artist.

Bill Figurski is not only Elfish's creator, he is also one of us— a Saint Vincent Engineering associate. Elfish was even designed and created at Saint Vincent in our offsite storage location. When the guys from engineering brought Elfish to the 25th Street entrance of the health center, a steady stream of associates came out to see him and to congratulate their long-time co-worker for his exceptional work. We're proud of Elfish Presley, we're proud of Bill, and we're proud to be a part of the GoFish! campaign."

Rebecca Gregory, Saint Vincent Health Center

Elfish Presley (singing Blue Suede Fins)
artist: Bill Figurski
patron: Saint Vincent Health Center
location: 232 West 25th Street

Whimsical Award
A fish full of fanciful fun
People's Choice 1st Place

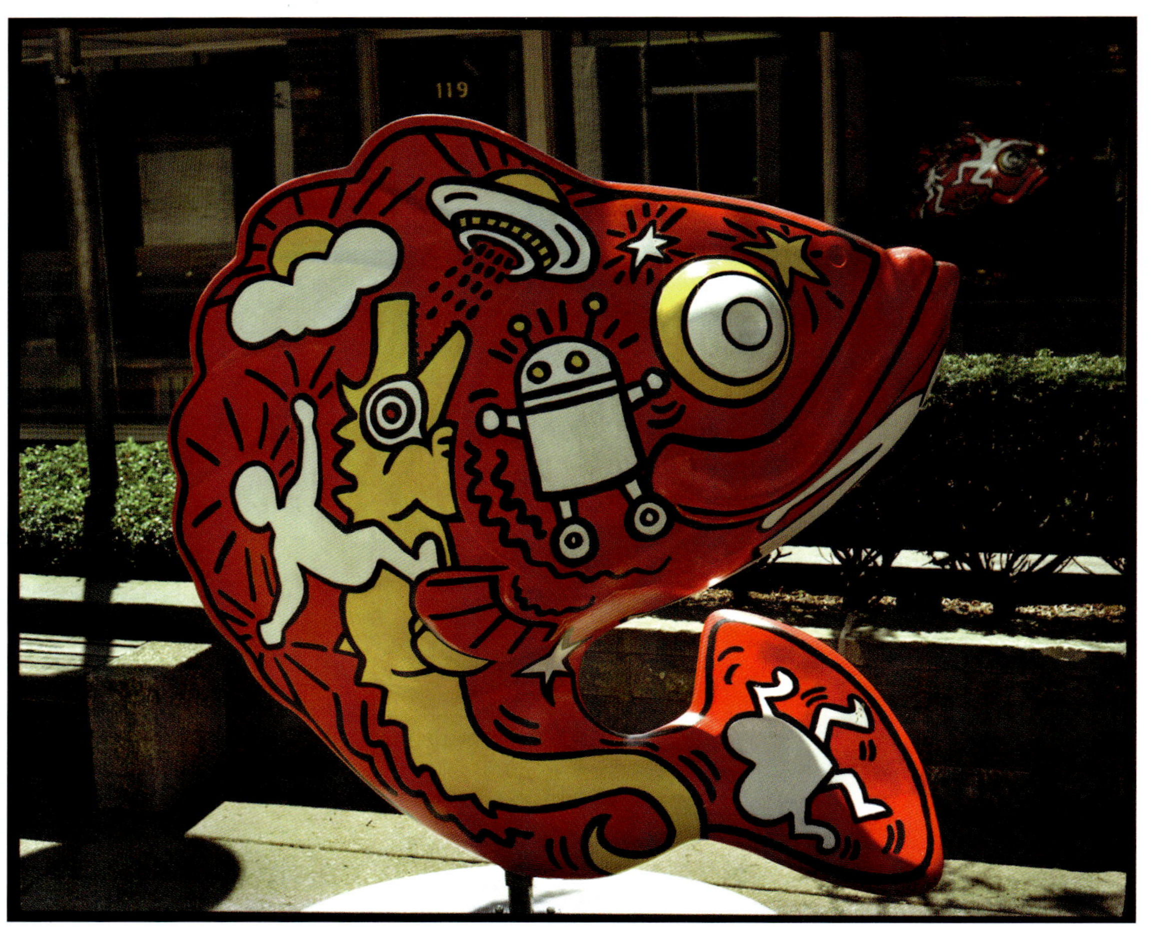

Red Haring
artists: Peggy Brace & Ed Roskowski
patron: Infinity Resources
location: 119 West 9th Street

encouragement fromhereand beyond

As herring is best when pickled, Keith Haring's work only improves with time. Haring was one of the first public street artists, drawing in chalk on blank subway ad spaces, so it's fitting that his designs be expressed on one of Erie's publicly-displayed fish. His style, abstract and presenting images as symbols, was well-researched by Peggy Brace, the fish artist. Peggy felt a strong connection with Haring, who died of AIDS in 1990; she received spiritual guidance from him— as well as from her son, whom she lost two years ago— while working on Red Haring.

She also listened to 11-year-old Zach Hess, the sponsor's grandson, when he voiced a request: the alligator-shaped monster was included just for him.

Ziegfeld Flounder
artist: Richard Davis
patrons: Erie Playhouse Wing, Erie Playhouse Board & Staff, Hagan Business Machines, Michelob Light & James F. Toohey
location: 13 West 10th Street

Child's Play Award
Full of color and fun for little ones

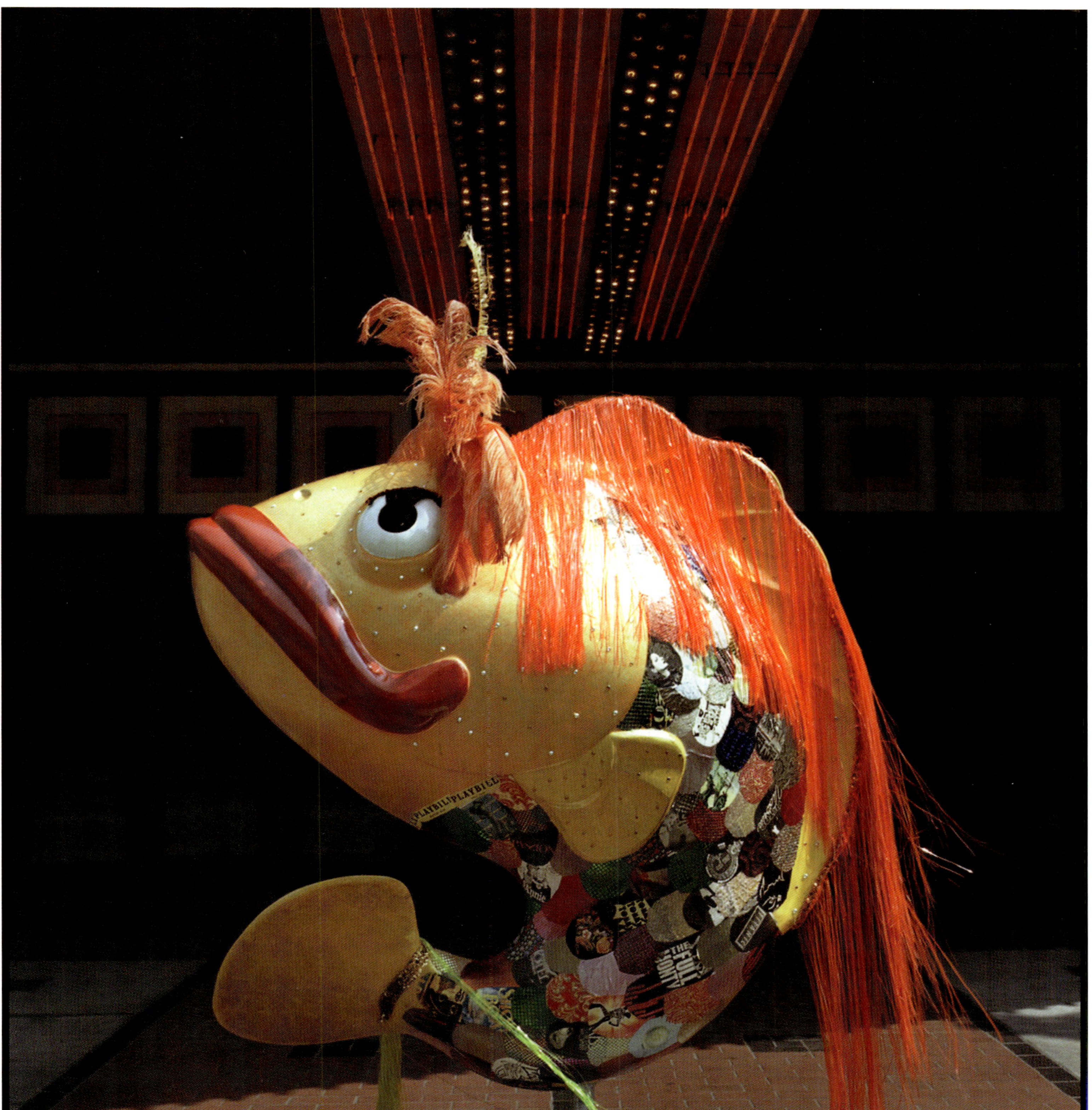
PLAYBILL PLAYBILL
THE FULL MONTY

"I have got to say that the fish are wonderful. They add sparkle to a city that can sometimes be a bit dreary. They put a smile on your face."

Suzanne
from Millcreek

notoneofthe koi-polloi

This fish ain't one of the bourgeoisie, no siree! First of all, it's done in gold leaf— that's right, not gold paint, but actual gold leaf. The gills are platinum and 22 karat gold, the main body is 23 karat gold, and the belly is 18 karat gold. Also, it was produced in the world-renowned Gold Leaf Studios in Washington, D.C., whose owner does work not only for the White House, but also for museums worldwide. *And*, when the Prince of Wales' right-hand man stopped by the studio while the artist was working, he raved about how he just loved the fish, and said, "I'm going to tell Charles about this!"

The Gillded Lily
artist: Abigail Adams Greenway
patron: G.L. Greenway II
location: 356 West 6th Street

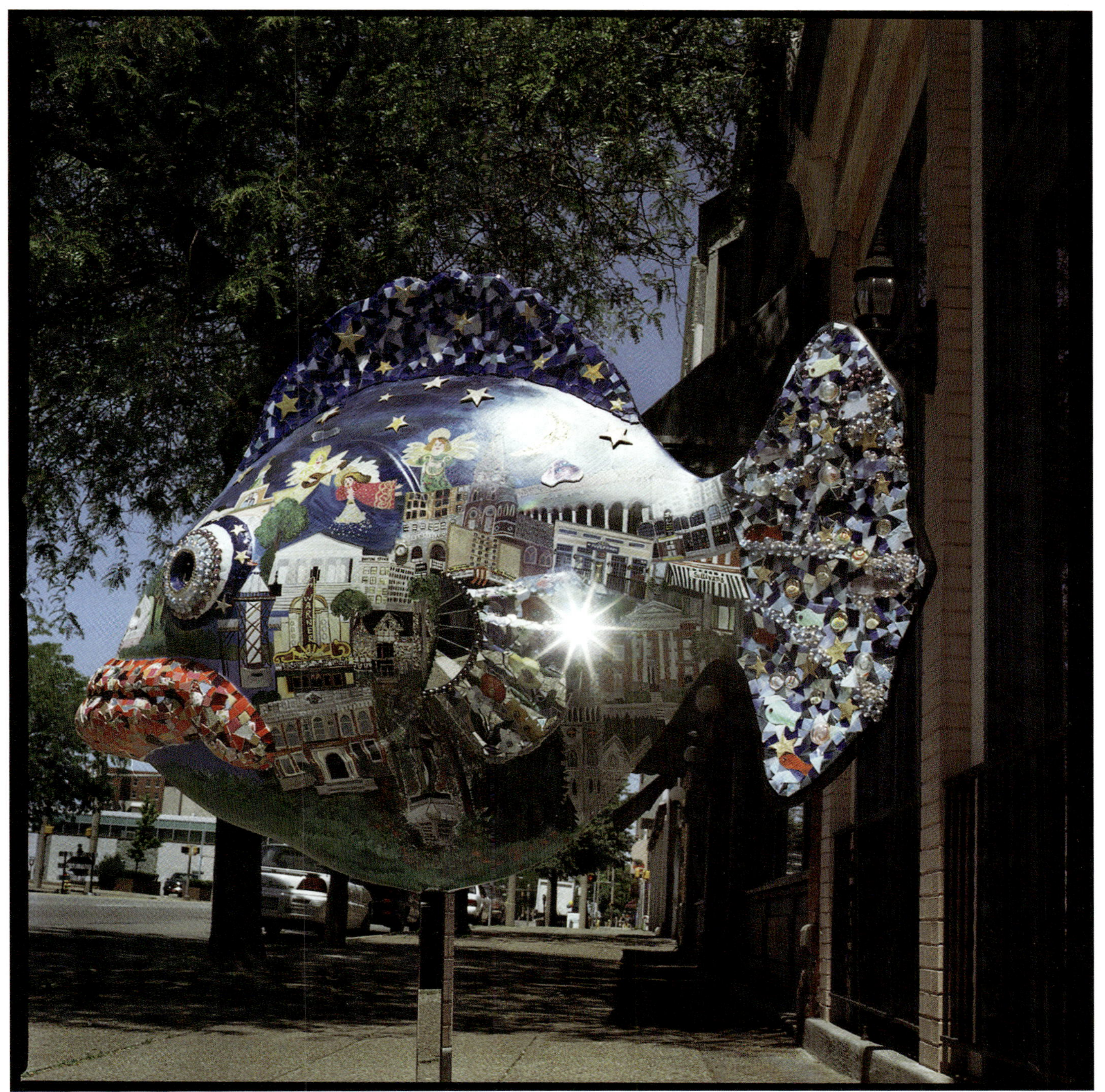

Fishkabibble
artist: Susan Moore
patrons: Perry Mill & papermoon
location: 14th & State Streets

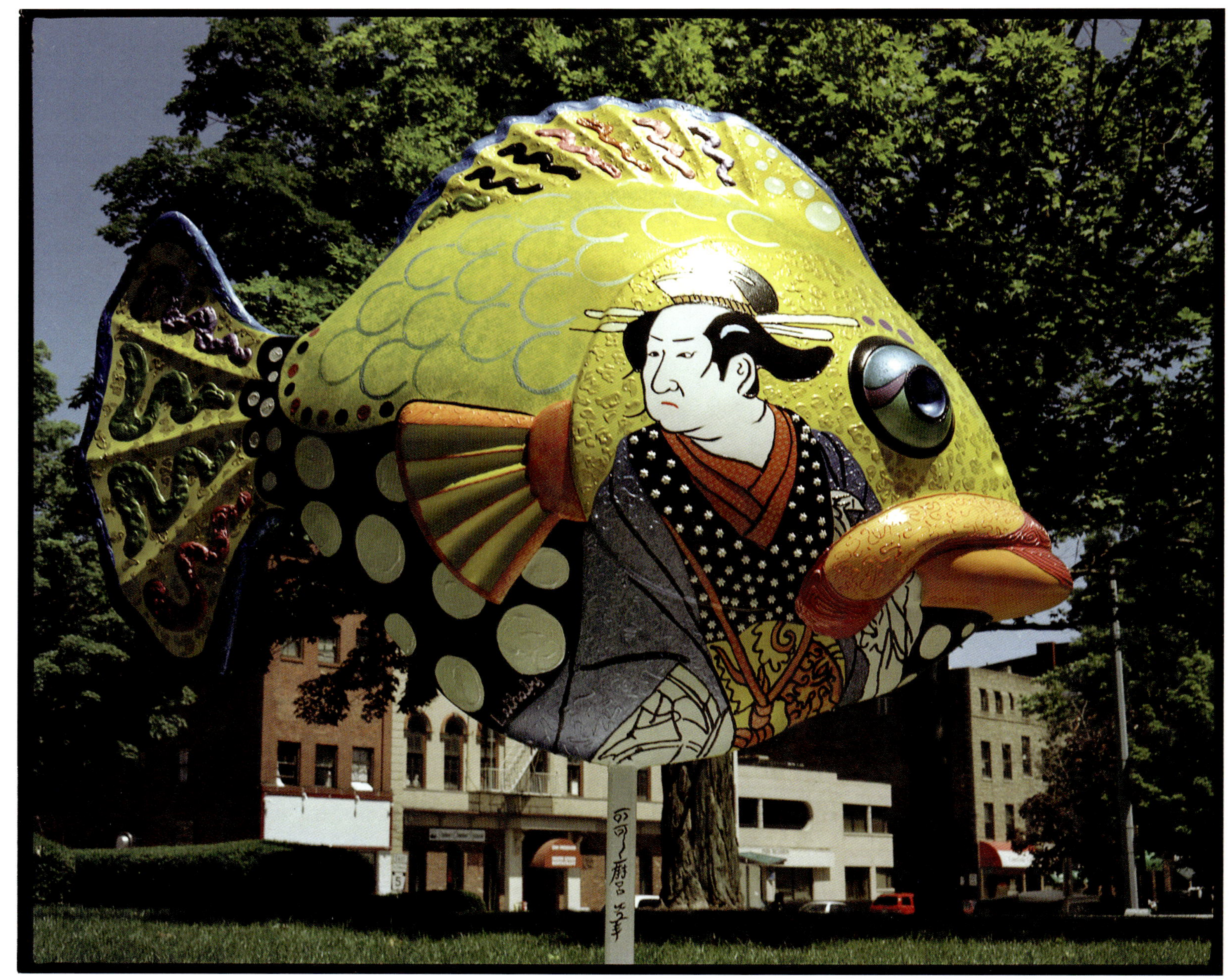

Juicy Sushi
artist: Brad Lethaby
patron: Gohrs Printing Service, Inc.
location: West 6th & Peach Streets
Most Artistic Award *A real museum gem*

sayitthreetimesfast

The goal: to use a lot of paint. Brad Lethaby, who usually creates portraits, was looking to do something less realistic and more fun. He wanted to use a lot of paint, making the fish "juicy," and decided that "sushi kind of rhymed with it."

His other goal was to include a big graphic image so it could be seen from a distance. An enthusiast of 17th century Japanese art, Brad drew inspiration from one of his favorite artists from the Kyoto School, Utamaro. In fact, the Japanese type on the base of the fish is Utamaro's name.

Some of the design, including the squiggles on the fins, was done with cake decorators that Brad borrowed from his friend Camille. (Please note, however, that this fish is made of neither sushi nor cake. While it is nice to look at, it is not tasty to eat.)

Food Fish
artist: Chuck Dill
patron: With Love to Ashley & Roxanne
location: East 12th & French Streets

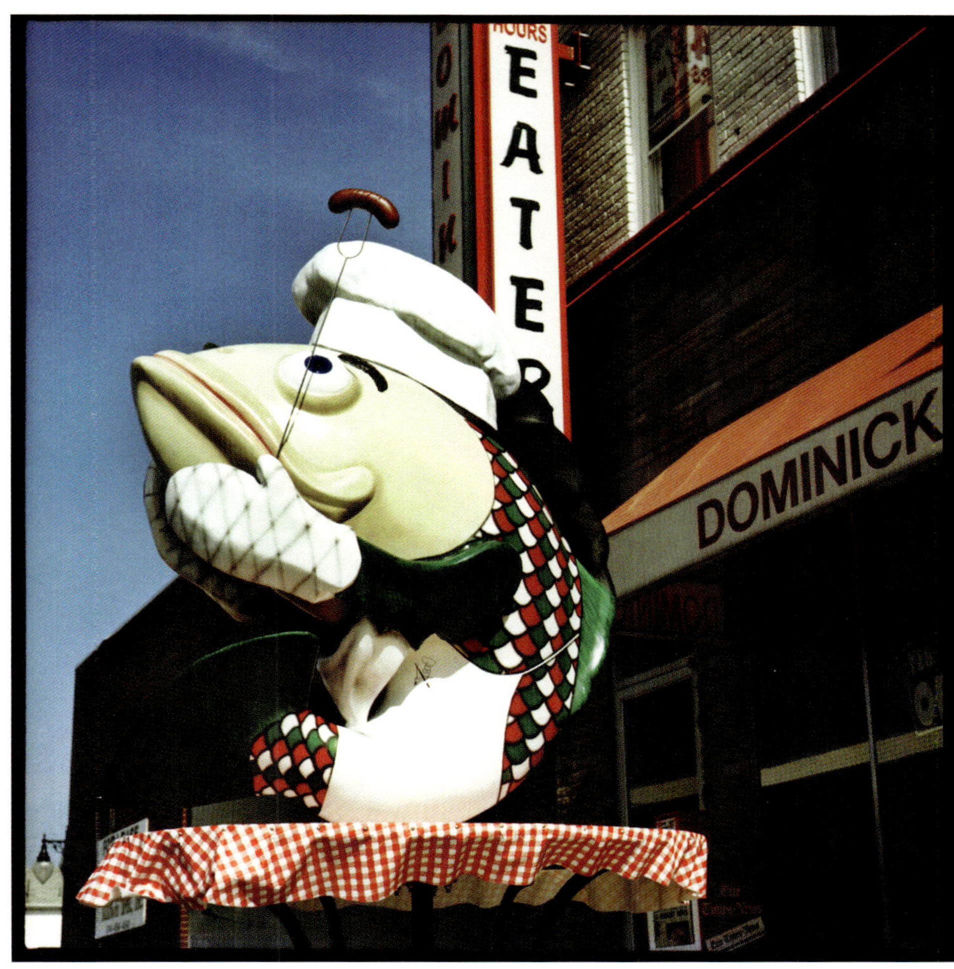

thestoriesofcatfishtales

by Hallie Mellon

In Strong Vincent's Catfish Tales, you will see something that very few of the other fish will have: the creation of an artwork by the ideas and talents of diverse individuals who are also students and educators of the School District of the City of Erie. Al and Peggy Richardson donated the fish to Strong Vincent High School. Being a part of Community Access Television (CAT), Al wanted the fish to reflect a theme of catfish. With that start, the students came up with the rest.

The students who participated in the project had their own tales to contribute to make this fish a part of who and what Strong Vincent is. The tiger portrait came from brainstorming and from a news story about the new tigers in the Erie Zoo. The movement from day-to-night and the metamorphosis of a catfish to a cat came from a poster and some very imaginative student minds. They are Allan Kavelish, Emily Gaudioso, Brian Boehm, Noe Latorre, Nelya Osmak, James Jasper, Darryl Jasper, Nicole Smith and Jessica Nixdorf.

An enormous amount of time was devoted to this project— over 850 hours from idea to completion. Students who did not have very much art experience came together to create a work that does not just have one designer, creator and doer, but many. In their efforts, they have succeeded in making themselves, their school and their city very proud.

"It is commonly known that communities can change schools. I have always subscribed to the idea that schools can change communities. 'Catfish Tales' has done just that. In 28 years of educational work, this project has been one of the most significant school-to-community collaborations I have seen."

Janet M. Woods, Principal, Strong Vincent

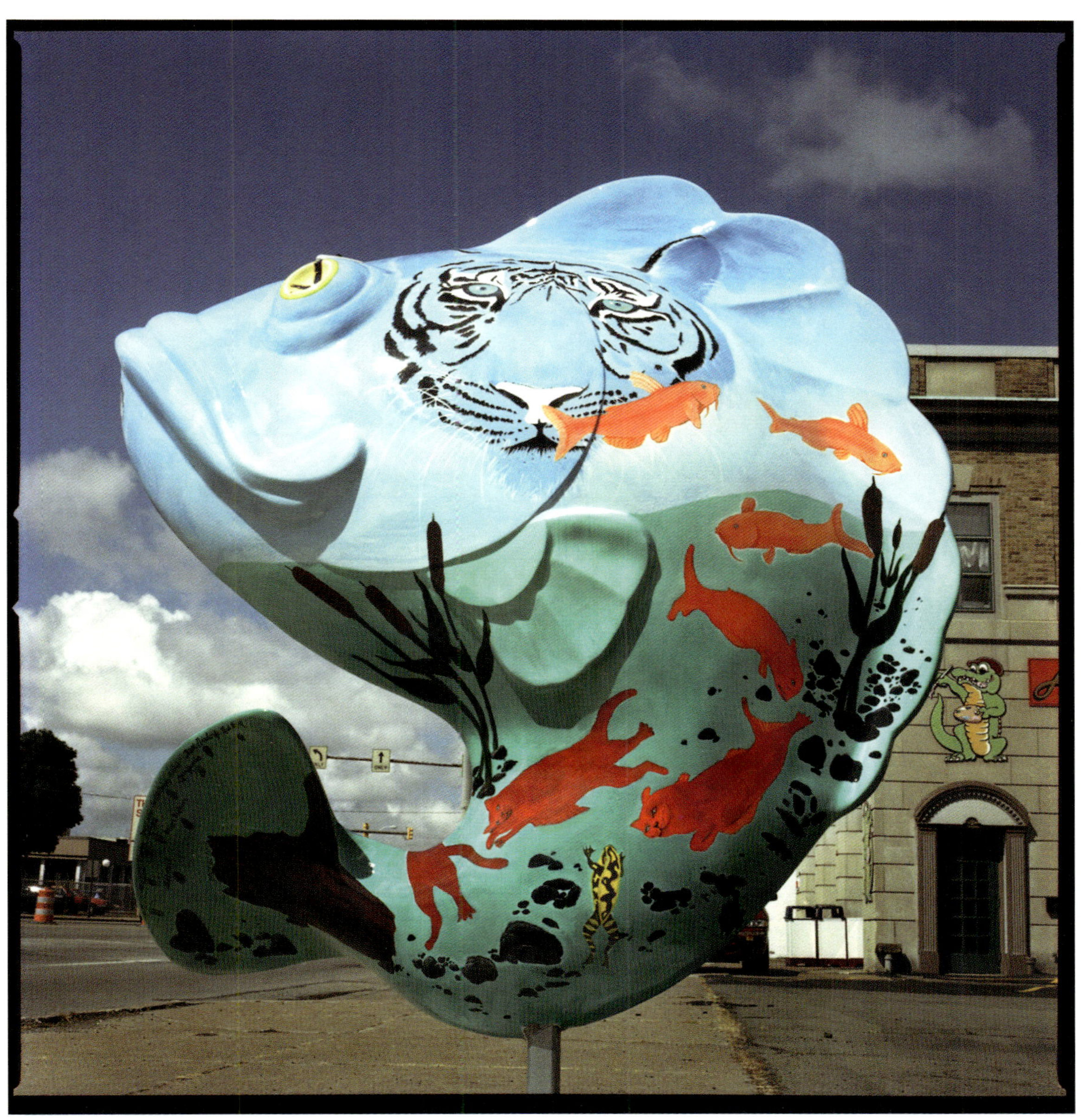

Catfish Tales

artists: Camille Dempsey-Nischal, Allan Kavelish, Emily Gaudioso, Brian Boehm, Noe Latorre, Nelya Osmak, James Jasper, Darryl Jasper, Nicole Smith, Jessica Nixdorf

patron: Al & Peggy Richardson

location: 142 West 12th Street

Team Effort Award

A collaborative fish, from start to finish

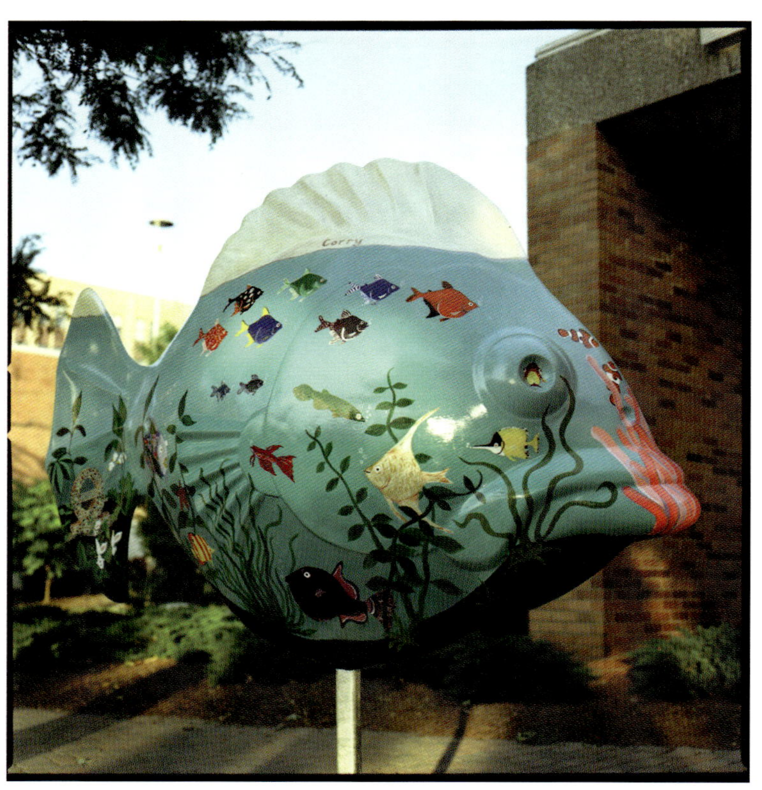

Corry Community Fishtank
artists: Christine Schalles & Kate Schalles
patrons: Christine Schalles, Roche Shamrock, LLC, Gerty White, Jane & Bill Roche, Corry Artists' Guild, Corry Area Art Council, Inc., Hoop & Marne Roche & Family
location: 143 West 7th Street

microCODsm/macroCODsm

Christine and Kate Schalles, one of three mother/daughter artist teams, made their fish into a miniature Corry, Pa. In an effort to showcase their hometown, they painted an aquarium where each individual fish represents some element of the community. An angelfish is dedicated to the 25+ churches in the Corry area, the American flag fish salutes the VFW and American Legion, the flying fish hails the Corry Lawrence Airport, and the rainbow trout represents the Corry Fish Hatchery, one of the oldest in the state.

The school of fish symbolizes the area schools in their colors, led by Corry High in orange and black. The Schalleses paid homage to the Corry Fine Arts Council with fish in the styles of Van Gogh and Picasso, and replicated the Rainbow Fish from the children's story to acknowledge the Corry library. And above the water level on both sides is a sunrise with the word "Corry" painted in it, to promise the town's bright future.

Oh— and by the way— some other fish were included just to make people wonder just what they represent.

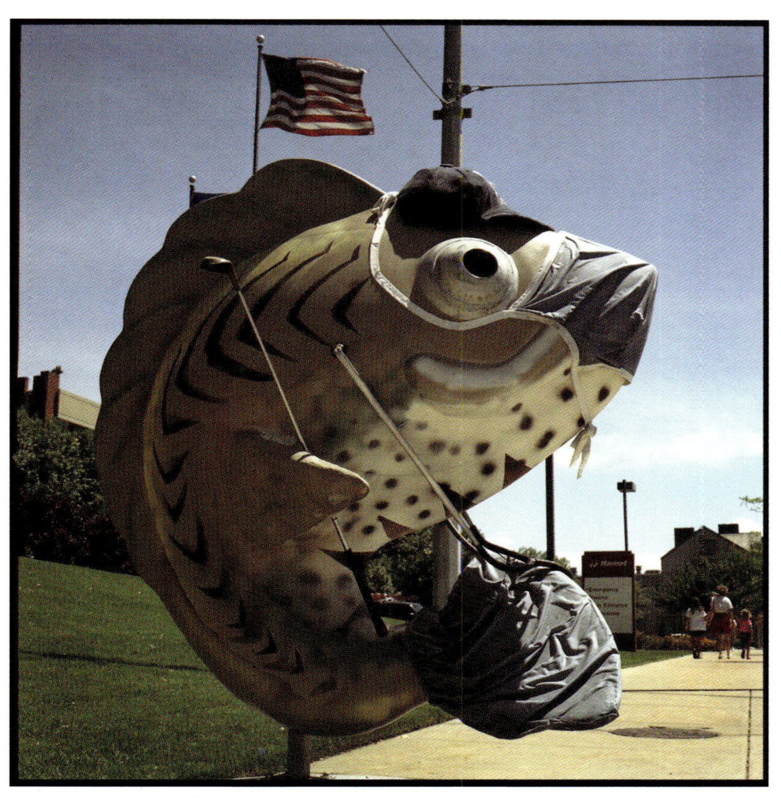

Dr. Sturgeon
artist: Bryan Toy
patron: Hamot Health Foundation
location: 201 State Street

Theme Award
Represents patron and location

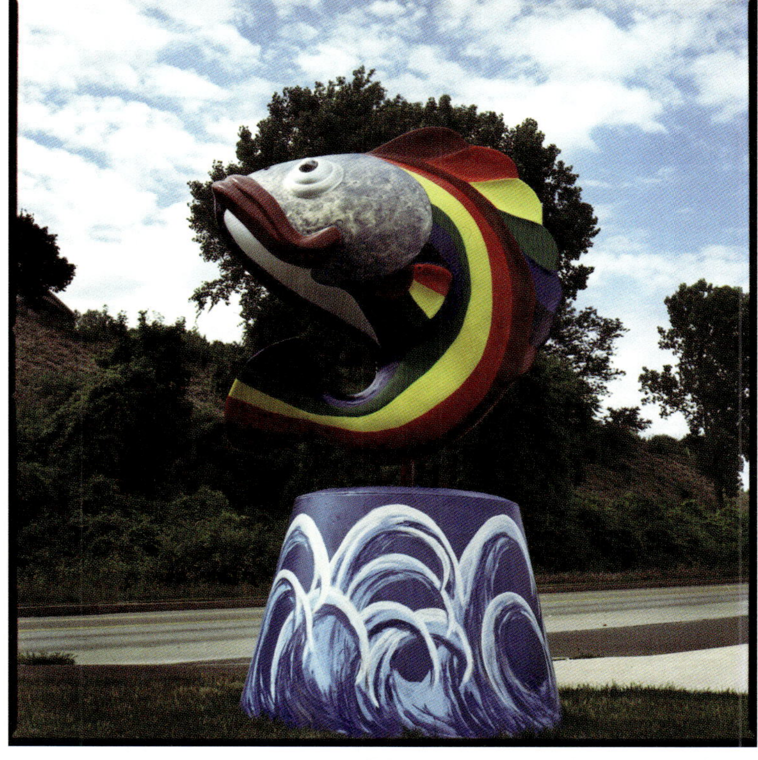

Ride the Wave–Catch the Gold
artist: Gay Kilmer
patron: Spectrum Control, Inc.
location: Bayfront Highway

nowthat'sitalian!

Artifishial
artist: Nancy E. Weaver
patron: Aurora Foods, Inc.
location: 2200 East 38th Street

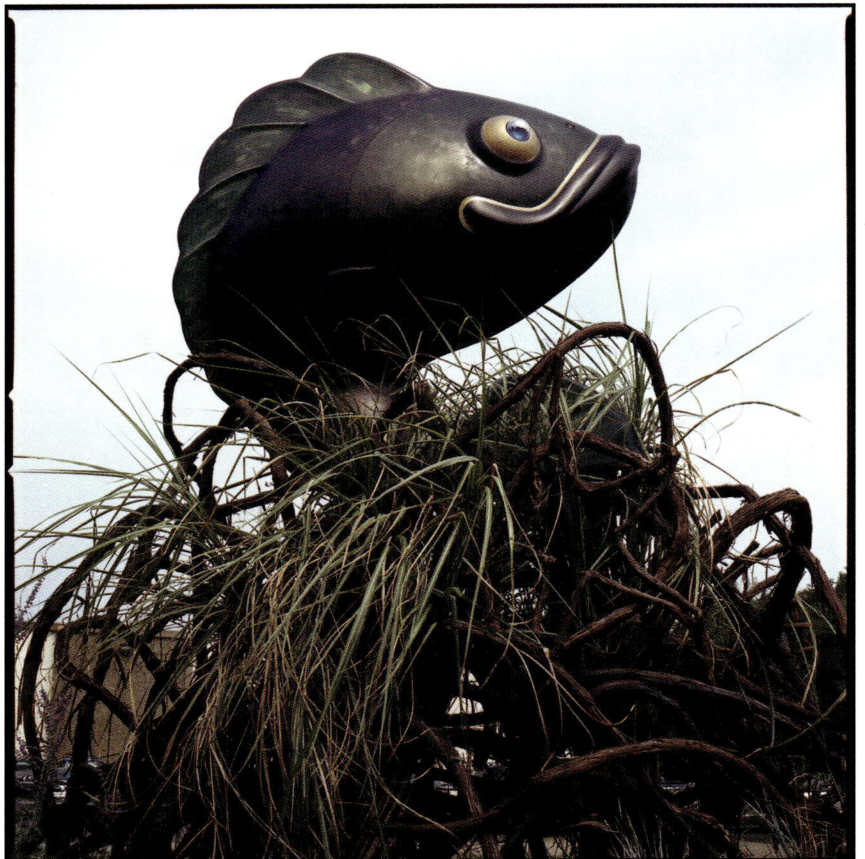

When Paul Gitnik refurbished the mansion in which his law firm is housed, he set aside the old copper gutters, and then asked Evan Everhart to incorporate them into his GoFish! fish. As Evan is an artist who works mostly in metal, he was thrilled to be able to add copper scales onto the fish's surface.

But, as part-time-artist-and-part-time-owner-of-a-creative-landscape-design-business, Evan didn't stop there. He poured concrete into the ground to hold the sculpture, raised far off the ground. He made a flower bed of silica pebbles and added subtle metal edging. And he even made his own plaque stand.

By the way, "Andiamo Pescare" means "let's go fish" in Italian. (Actually, it doesn't— they found out later that the spelling is just slightly off, but only the very well-versed in Italian might pick up on it.) Which is apt, since sponsor Gitnik was born in Italy.

"Everyone I talk with thinks this is just the greatest fun. We're like little kids when we spot one we haven't seen before, and share with each other which way to drive home from work to see a new one!"

Judith Oncea

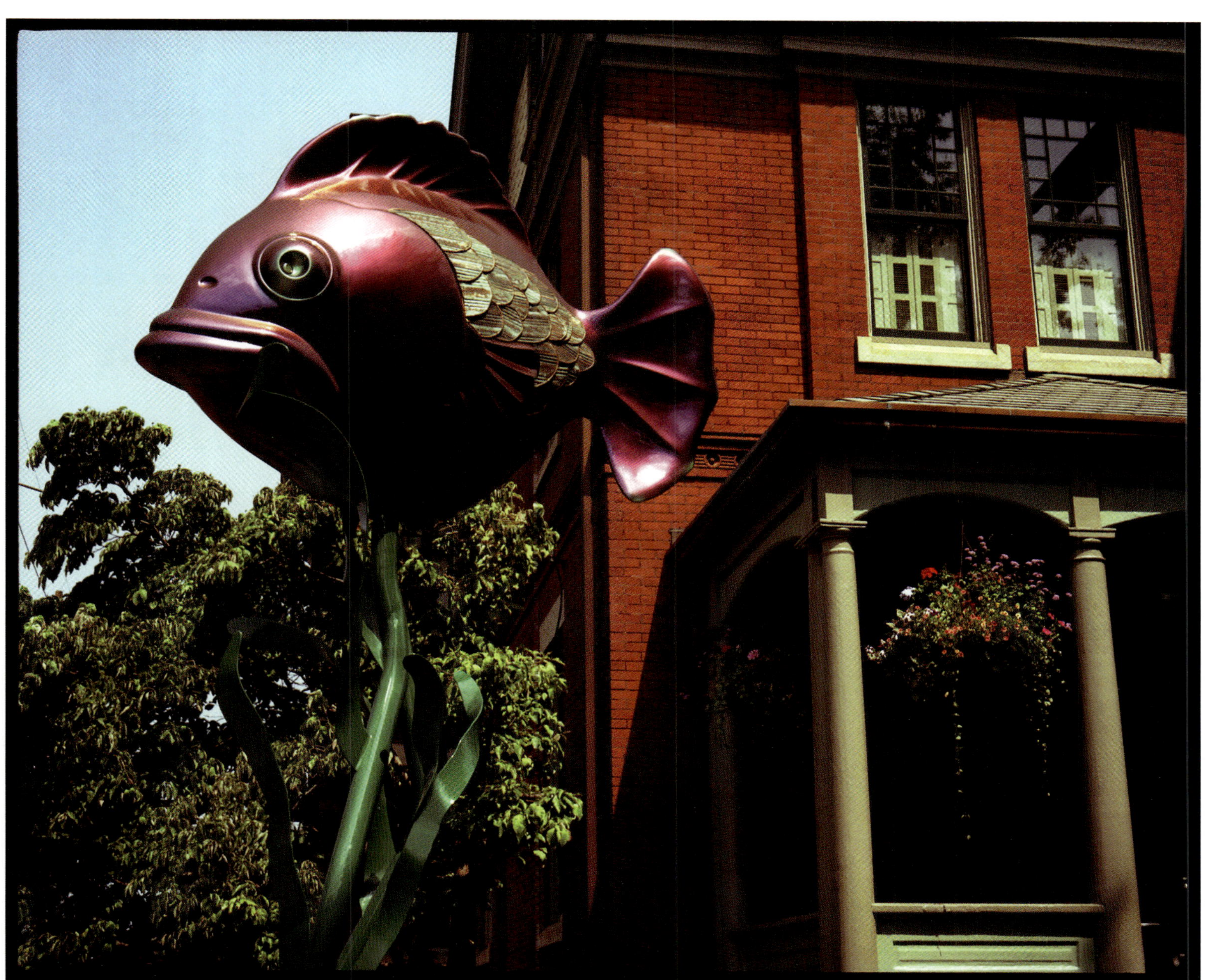

Andiamo Pescare
artist: Evan K. Everhart
patron: Paul Gitnik & Associates, LLC
location: West 6th & Sassafras Streets
Photogenic Award *An attractive catch*
People's Choice 2nd Place

(*The answers are: The newspaper. A blushing zebra. A sunburnt zebra. A baby penguin with diaper rash. A penguin holding its breath. A Dalmatian with chickenpox.)

What's Black & White & Read (Fish) All Over?*
artist: Ken Wyten
patron: Erie Times-News
location: West 12th & Sassafras Streets

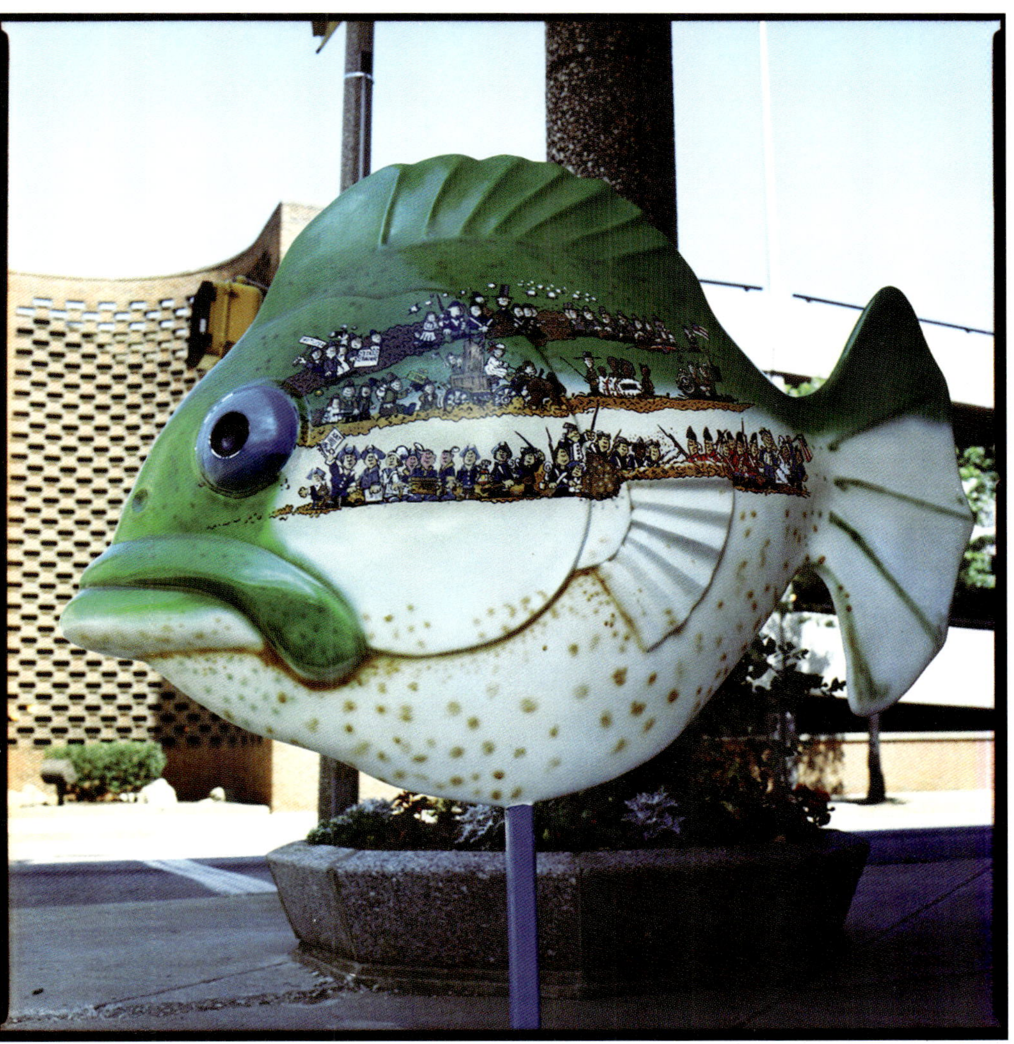

funwiththeboss

Bob Smith originally wanted to call this yesteryear-themed fish "The Giant Crappie of History." But after approaching Hoop Roche—his sponsor *and* his boss—with the idea, he agreed that the moniker Fishtorical Perspective might be less controversial.

At the time he was brainstorming fish ideas, Bob's son Kevin was taking American History in school, so he decided to put together historical elements that children could both see and recognize. On one side, he depicted the Revolutionary War through the Civil War. On the other, he portrayed the Civil War through the present. He included a painting of his father, Harold Smith, a chief warrant officer who served in WWII from '39-46, which is why the words "For Dad" are written on the sculpture.

Bob Smith surrendered The Giant Crappie, but he did get his fun in: not only do images of Hoop and his wife Marne appear in the immigration scene, Hoop is also portrayed in another spot, bemoaning Prohibition.

Fishtorical Perspective
artist: Bob Smith
patron: Erie Plastics
location: West 8th & Peach Streets

"Great photo op! Outstanding art to be enjoyed by young an

Loretta R. Baran (retired teacher of the deaf)

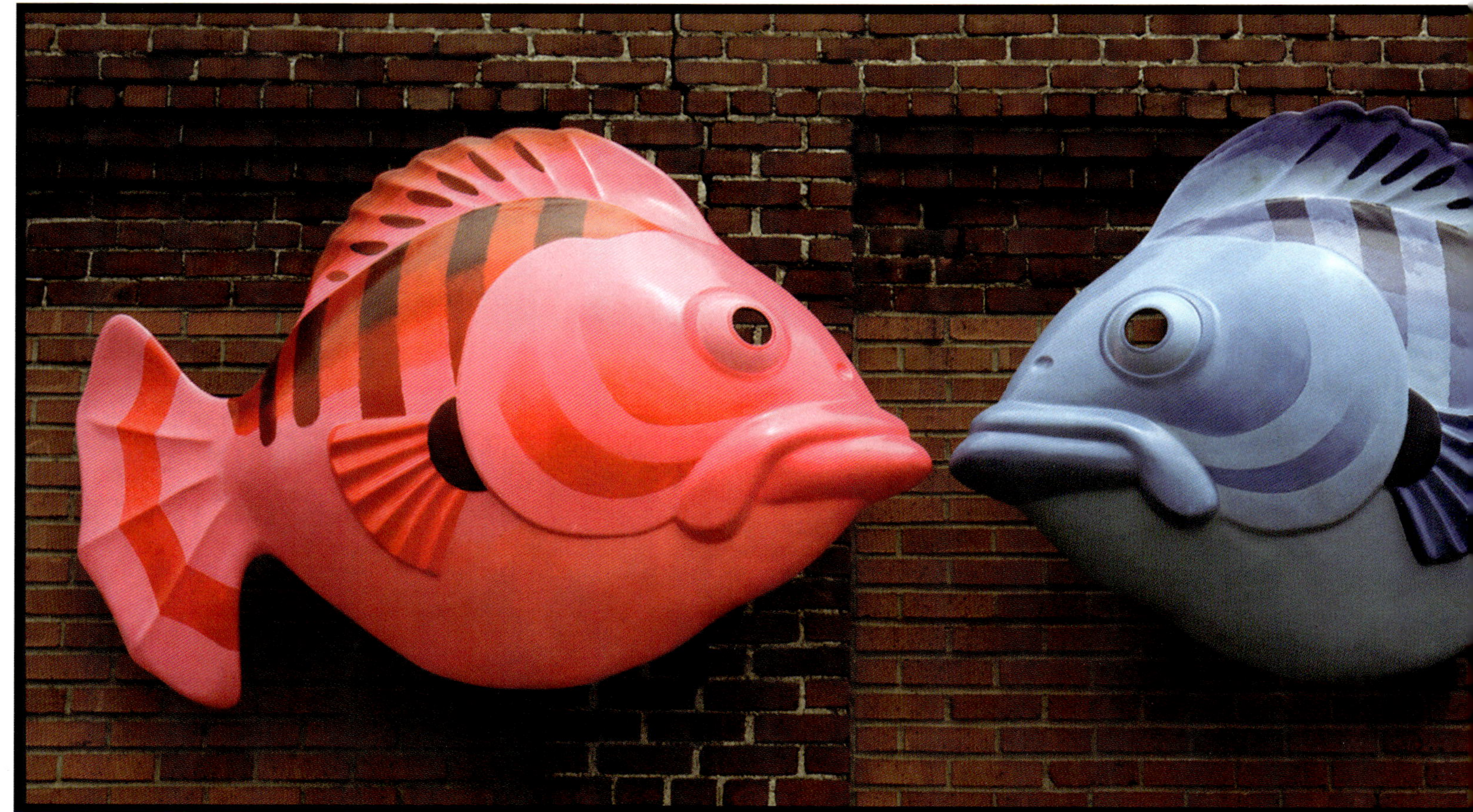

Kissing Fish
artist: Francis T. Schanz
patron: Dovetail Gallery
location: East 18th & Parade Streets

d alike!"

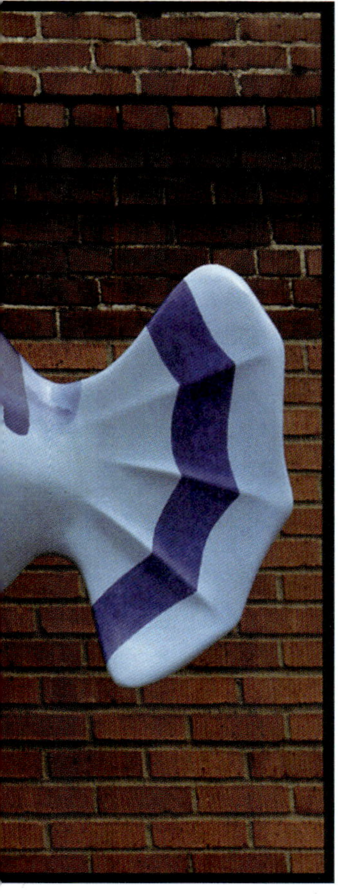

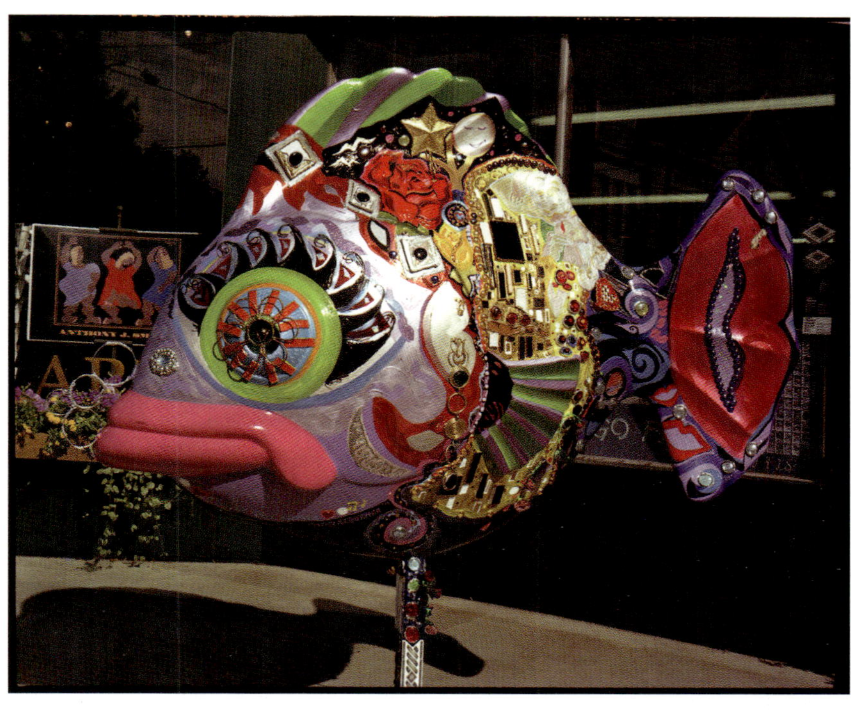

Fish Kiss
artist: Cynthia M. Christopher
patron: U-Frame-It & The Poster Annex
location: West 8th & Liberty Streets

abigsmackeroo

Cynthia Christopher is adamant that she didn't actually replicate anything. But, as great admirers of the artist Gustav Klimt, Matt Lebowitz and Phyllis Mashyna asked their artist to draw inspiration from Klimt in designing their fish. So, on this sculpture, there is an ever-so-subtle interpretation of Klimt's most celebrated painting "The Kiss"—not even discernible on a drive-by, something you have to get up close to see—incorporated in with some of his patterns. Adding texture to fish are mixed media elements such as glass, tile, mirrors, jewels, silk roses, copper, aluminum and even paper.

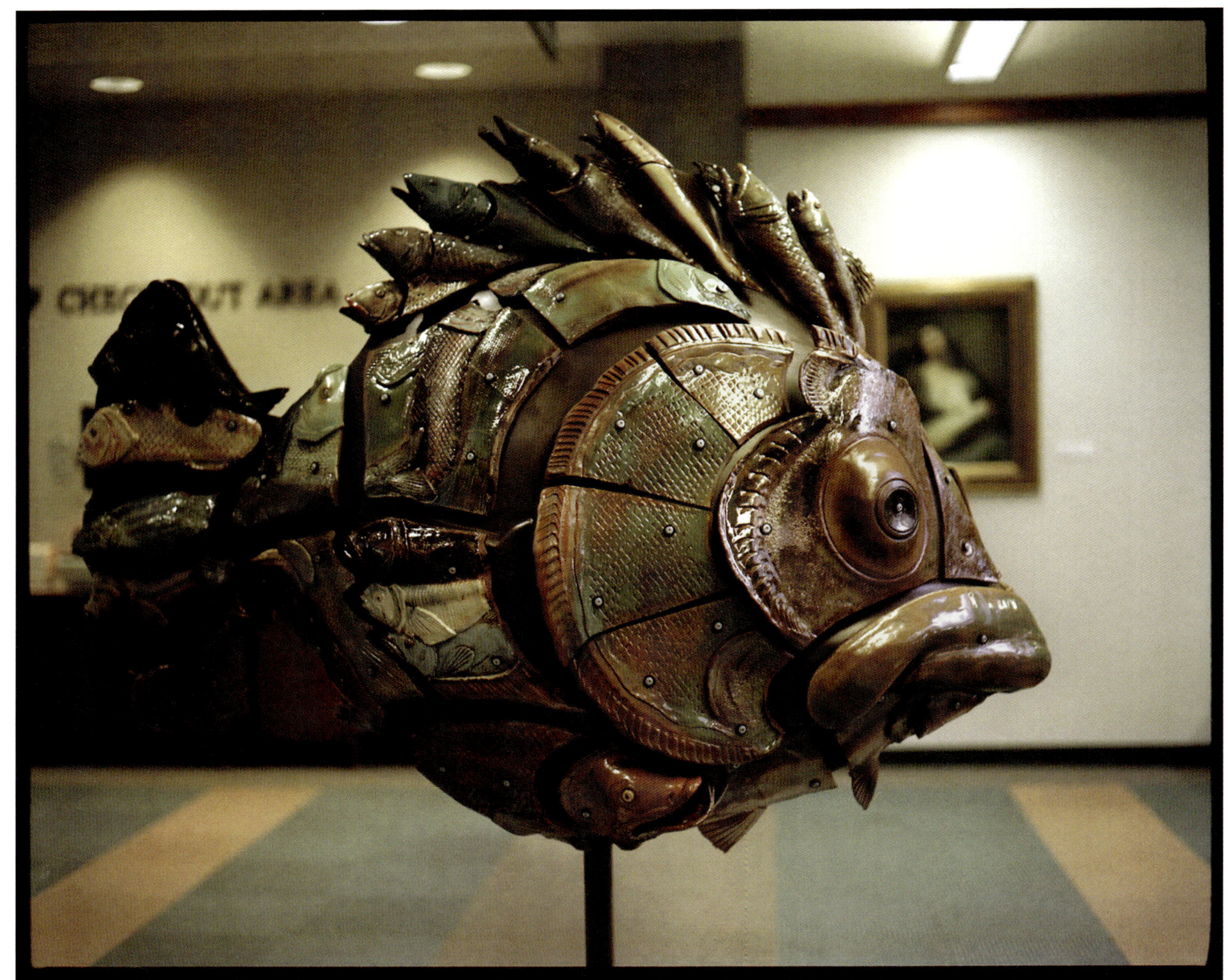

Baked Fish
artist: Tom Hubert
patron: Printing Concepts
location: Library Lobby, 160 East Front Street
The Angler's Award *A real trophy fish*

afavoriteinschoolcafeterias

Tom Hubert (who is not a cafeteria lady but has been the director of Mercyhurst College's art department for nine years) went through 400 pounds of clay in creating Baked Fish.

Determined to include representations of as many local fish as possible, this artist did extensive research on the fish of Erie's waterways. He studied up on fish such as yellow pike and walleye, perch and catfish, rainbow trout and bluegills. He played with different textures, toyed with various shapes and experimented with multiple styles.

This gave fish different facial expressions, creating individual personalities for each of the 37 fish on Baked Fish.

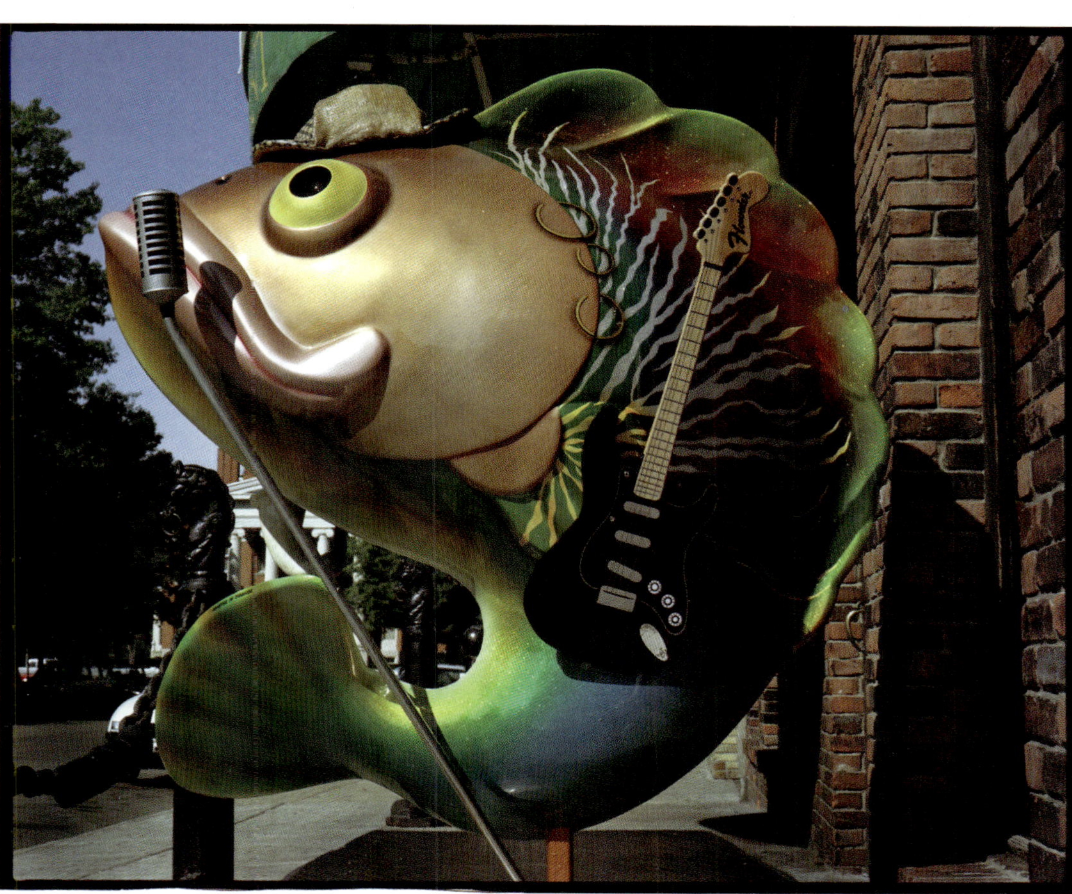

Sherrock
artists: Cathy Hahn & Greg Felix
patron: Sherlock's/Park Place
location: North Park Row

Theme Award
Represents patron and location

justlikechristmas

Mary Pat Lynch didn't just stop at creating a watercolor-quilted fish made with designer fabric samples provided by an interior decorator friend. Not even close. Instead, this manager of the Giant Eagle at Yorktown Center photo lab set up an entire system wherein a person who brought in film containing GoFish! photos to be developed would be deemed a Fish Finder and receive free photo-related prizes.

"Everybody has fish in their film," Mary Pat said. "Like everyone has their Christmas tree in their film."

To help her customers on their fish-finding missions, Mary Pat, a longtime photographer herself, created a display of enlarged fish photos. She even put together a corresponding binder with additional information on artists, locations, etc.

Mary Pat credits the owner of her Giant Eagle store as being "very generous, and very community-minded," in allowing her such latitude.

In fact, she even mixed the epoxy for her own fish in Giant Eagle deli containers.

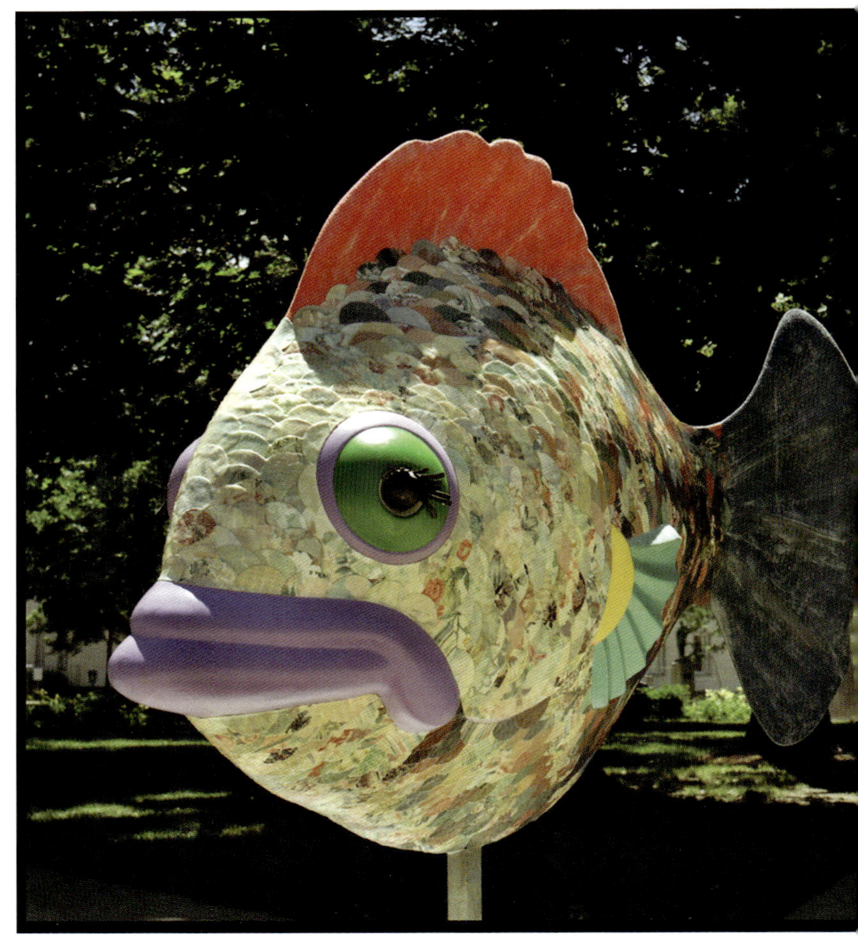

Lake Erie La
artist: Mary Pat Lyn
patron: Giant Eag
location: Perry Square, French Street
North Park R

orangeyougladit'ssafe?

Nothing's going to happen to *this* fish. First of all, Mary Kay Geary's three eldest children, aged 17, 23 and 25, have dedicated themselves to doing drive-bys, patrolling, making sure everything's okay with Ray of Hope.

Second, there is a gentleman who lives in Schmid Towers. He is quiet and doesn't speak any English, but sits on the bench near the fish and watches it, like its own guardian angel.

And third, there is the steady traffic of children playing the 24 Carrot game, poring over every inch of the fish to find the two dozen orange root vegetables hidden in its design.

(By the way, for those who can't find all 24...the last two are in the eyes.)

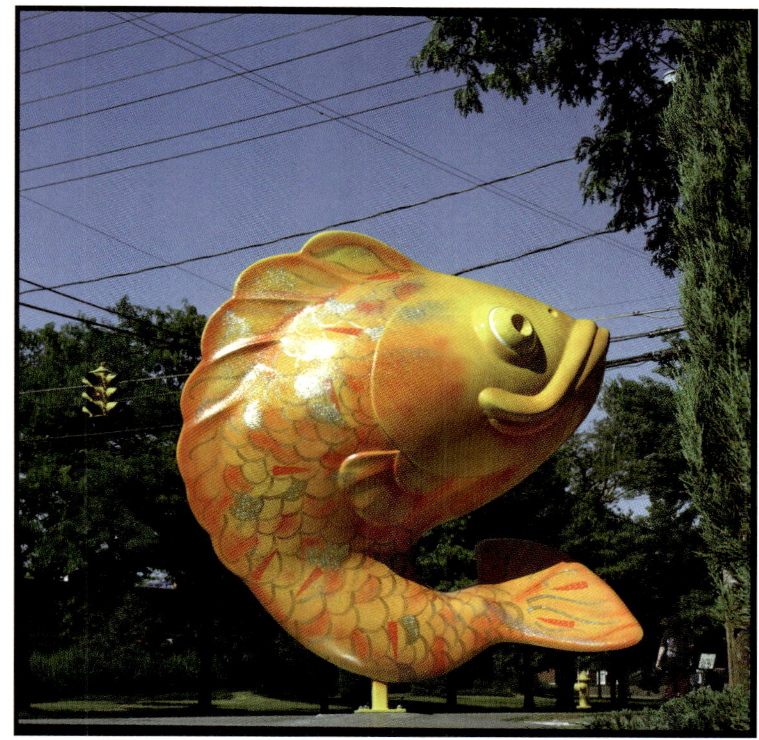

Ray of Hope, 24 Carrot Goldfish
artist: Mary Kay Geary
patron: Erie Housing Authority of the City of Erie
location: East 6th & Holland Streets

"I went to Giant Eagle in the Yorktown Plaza to buy a GoFish! T-shirt. The woman who sold it to me was Mary Pat Lynch, creator of 'Lake Erie Lady,' one of the fish located by the fountains downtown. She talked to me about how she made her fish. Boy, was I amazed. I like her fish because it is colorful."

Nichole Justka, age 10, St. Boniface School

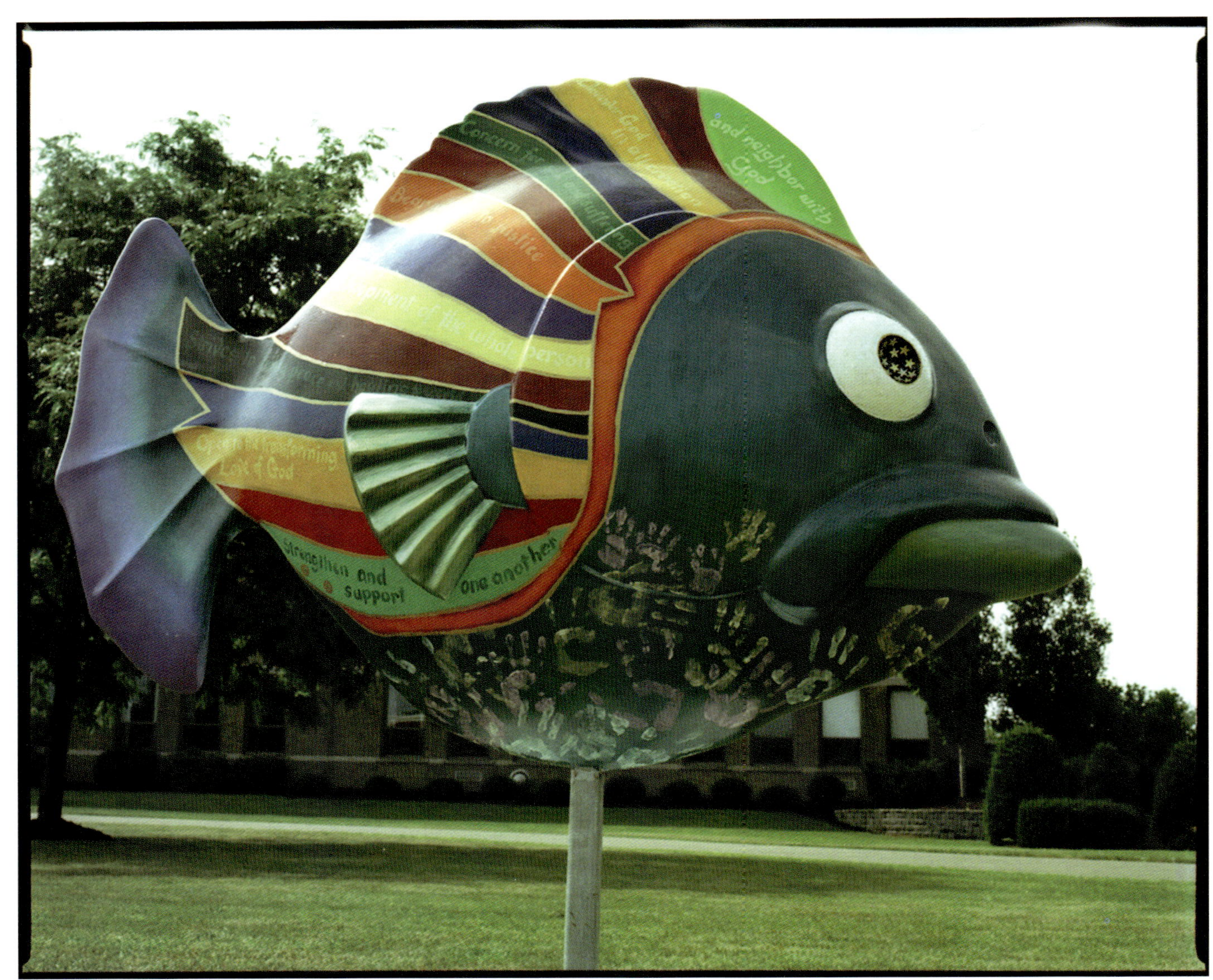

The Sisters of St. Joseph and the Amazing Technicolor Dream Fish

artist: The Sisters of St. Joseph with assistance from art teachers and students from Villa Maria Academy

patron: PNC Financial Services Group

location: 2403 West 8th Street

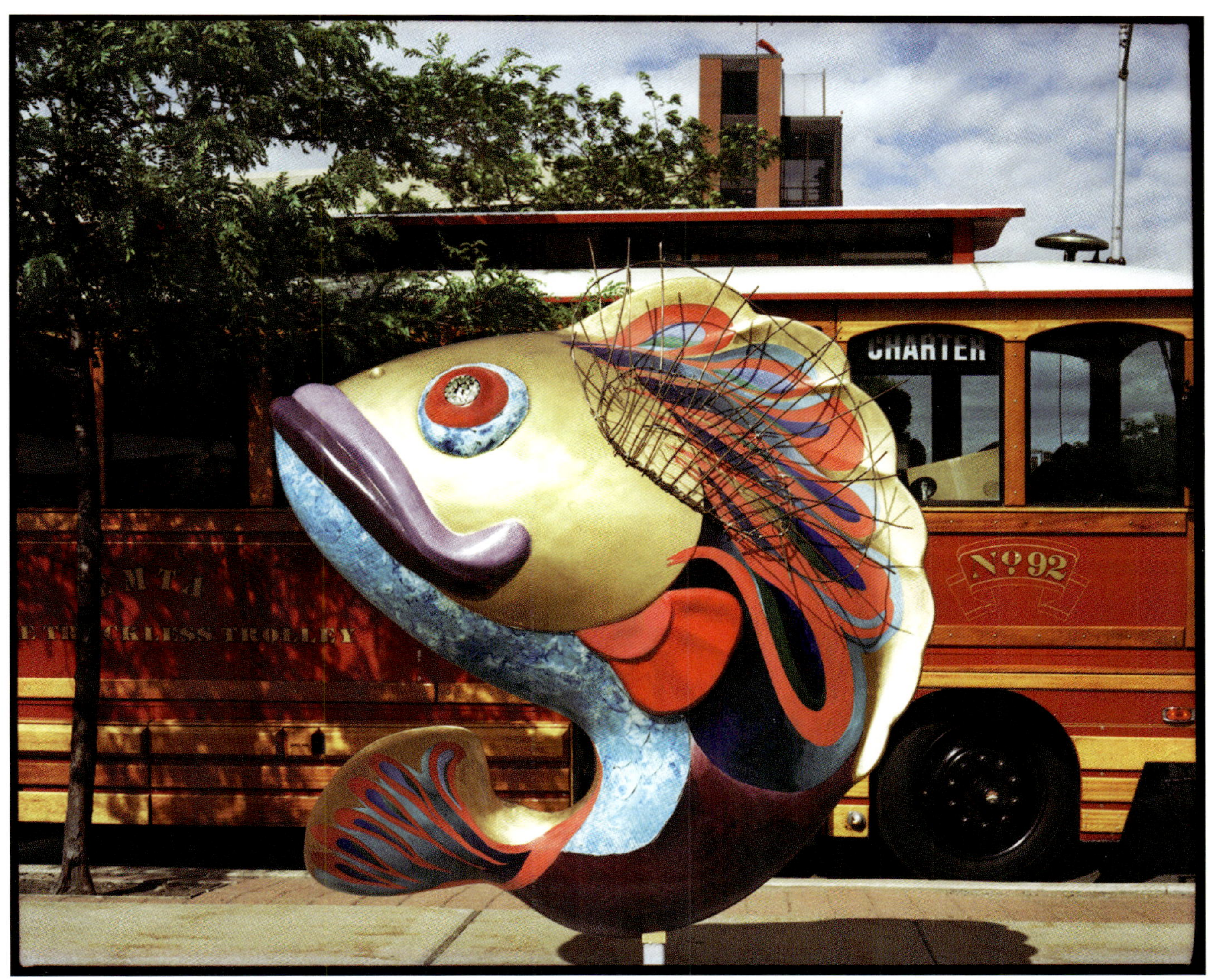

Red Wing
artists: Annoel & Peggy Krider
patrons: Mr. & Mrs. Henry Fish & Family
location: 3rd & State Streets

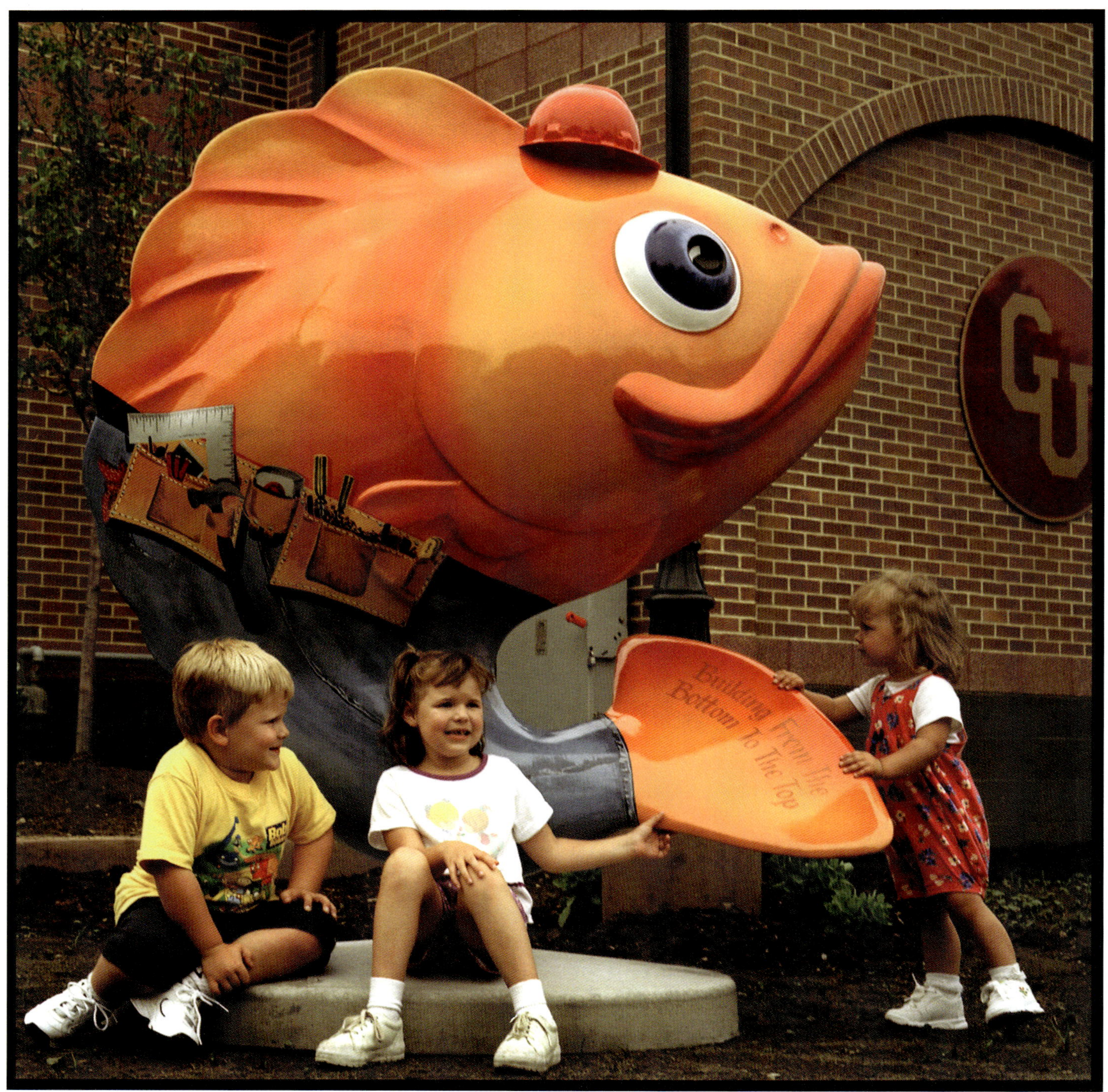

Carpenter Carp
artist: Kim Narcisco
patron: Jim & Joan Schaaf, Building Systems, Inc.
location: West 5th & Sassafras Streets

"Today, Wednesday, July 25 we had a GoFishWest33rd party. Almost all of the children from the 100 block gathered in my garage and made their own fish to decorate the block. The 19 children used large sheets of Styrofoam for the form of the fish. Then they decorated them with paint, beads, pompoms, bows, yarn, buttons, Popsicle sticks, and glitter. They did a great job, and when their fish was finished, they had a fishing snack: goldfish, Swedish fish, and pretzel fishing rods. We had a fun afternoon fishing."

Toni Dillon, school teacher

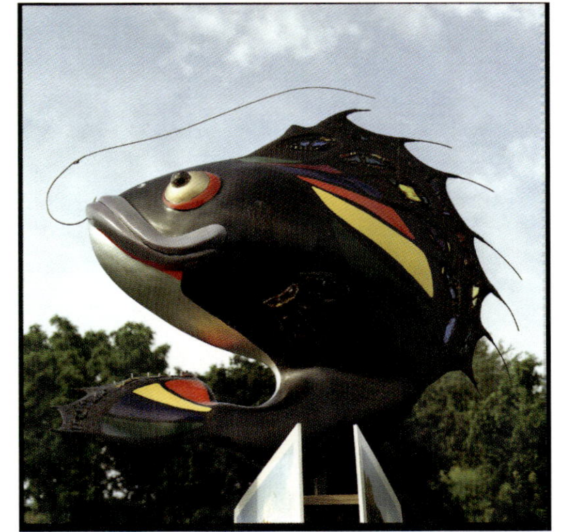

Stained Glass Bass
artists: Ed Grout & Creators from the Black Lagoon
patron: One Liberty, LLC
location: Bayfront Highway

The Wave–After Hokusai
artist: Roy Ahlgren
patron: Country Fair, Inc.
location: Country Fair Playground at Liberty Park Amphitheater

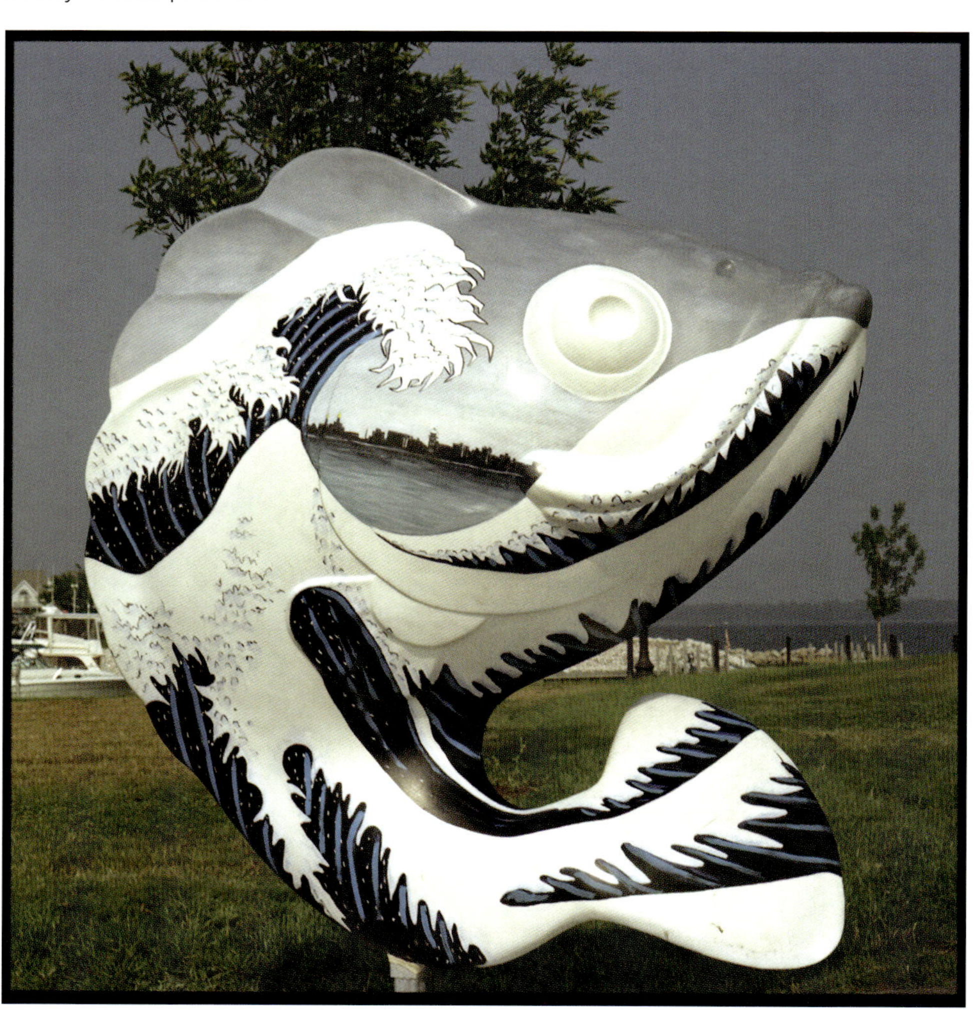

thanksfortheshower,roy

Summer of 2001 was the driest one in 85 years. Not since July 1916, when Erie received .39 inches of rain, has Erie had a drier summer.

Which is why we give a big thanks to Roy Ahlgren, for recreating the 1831 Katsushika Hokusai woodblock print The Great Wave Off Kanagawa (Fugaku sanjurokkei: Kanagawaoki namiura) on his fish.

Since he thought it would tie in well with this piece— the waves, the waterfront— Roy decided to create his own interpretation. He simplified it, set the wave off to make it appear more prominent, and added our local skyline...essentially, he lifted the gigantic wave from the print and set it down in Erie.

It didn't help make the grass any greener, but it sure did feel good coming down!

Lost on the Koi Sea
artist: William T. Anysz
patrons: Erie Arts Council, Mary Alice Doolin, Tom Doolin, Geri Cicchetti, & The Erie Zoo
location: The Erie Zoo

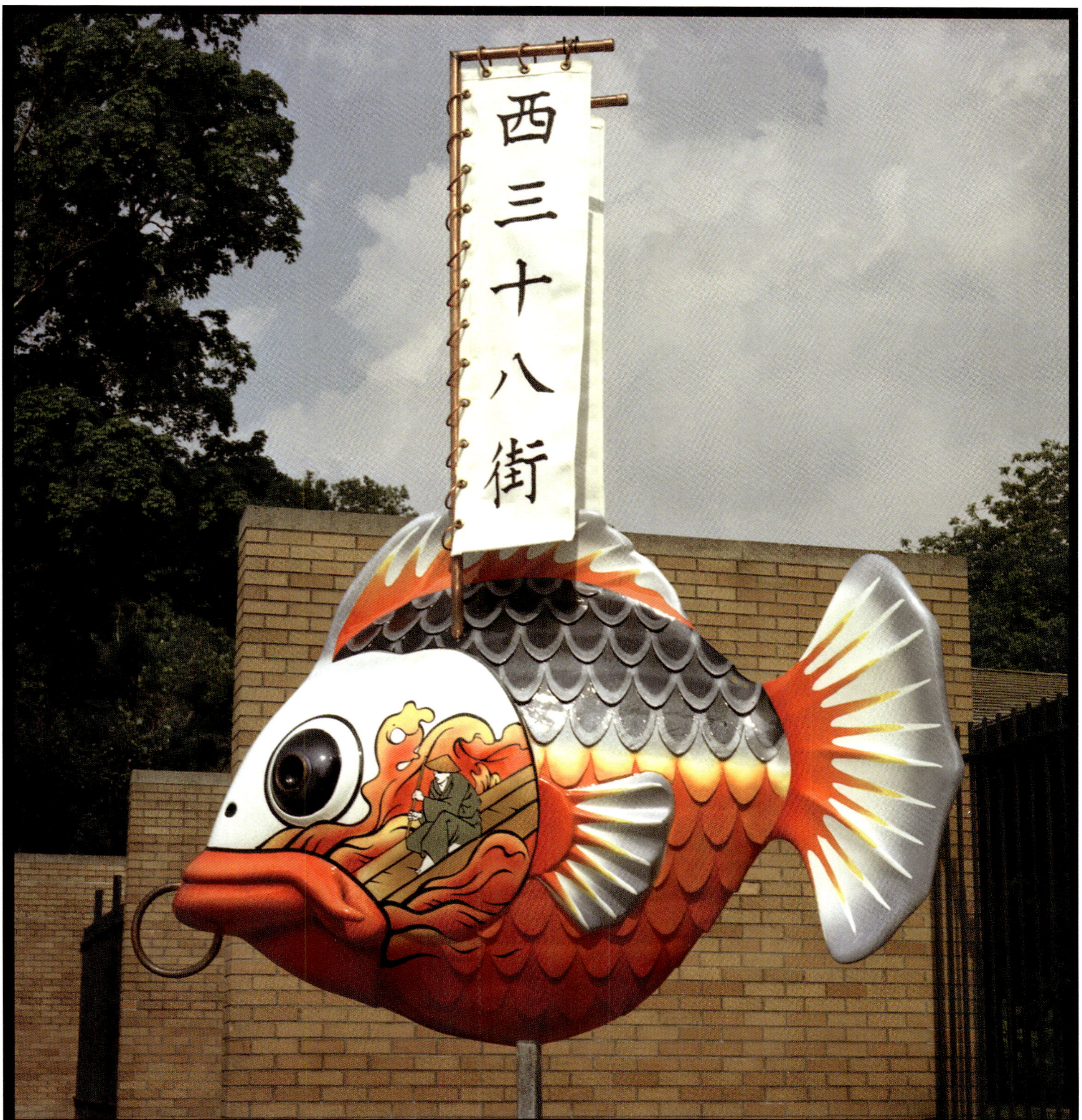
西三十八街

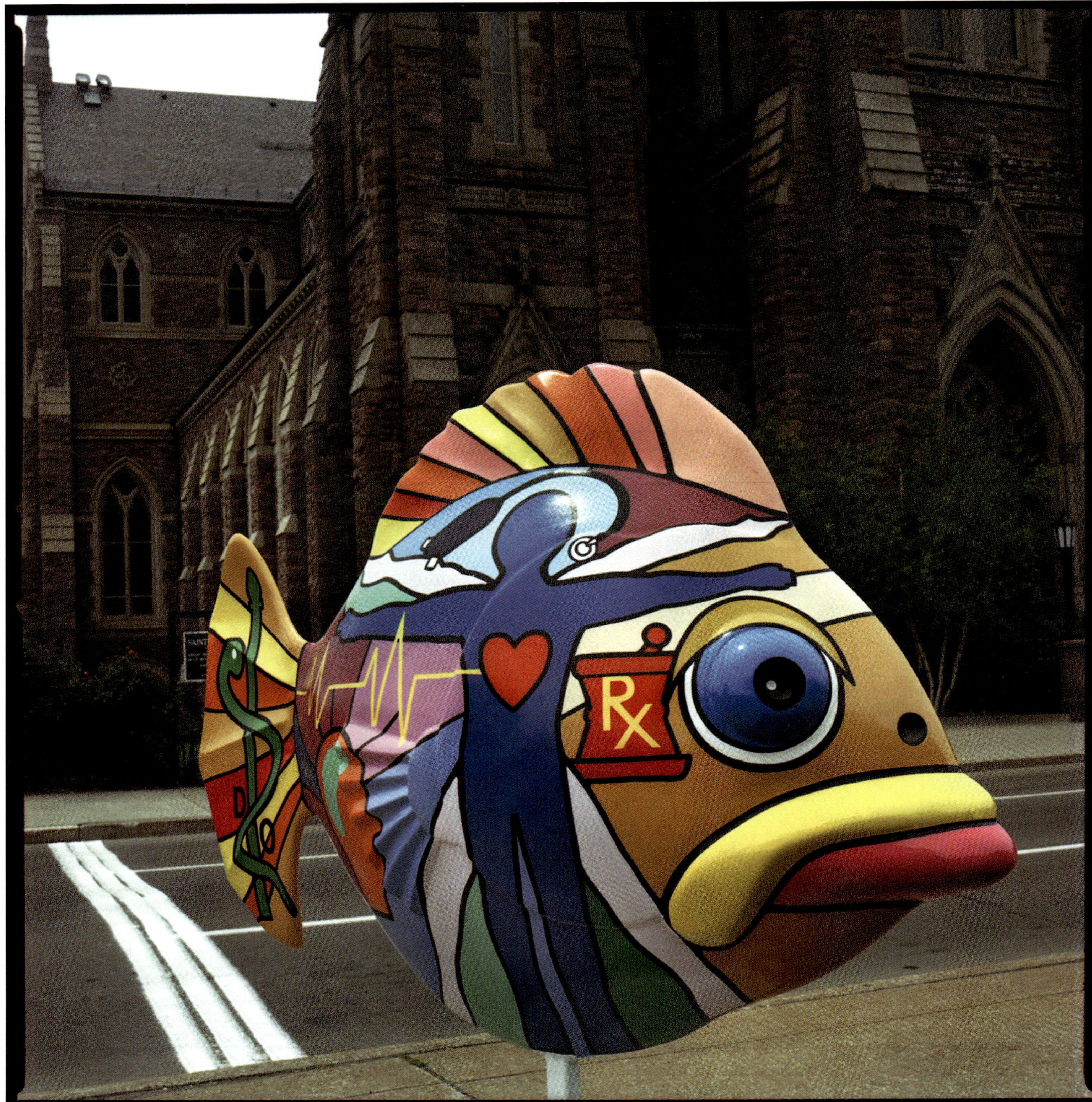
Rx

thebigfishnapping

What's interesting about the abduction of the Sturgeon General is not who took it, or how, or when or even why. It was the community's reaction.

The fish was reported missing by a number of different sources, by people who hoped that it was just in for repairs and then realized that it had been stolen. But within hours, a memorial shrine had been erected on its forlorn base. It was covered with yellow bows and ribbons, flowers, candles and even a stuffed fish. The fire department brought their own plywood fish over to serve as proxy and left a sign: "Who has the fish?"

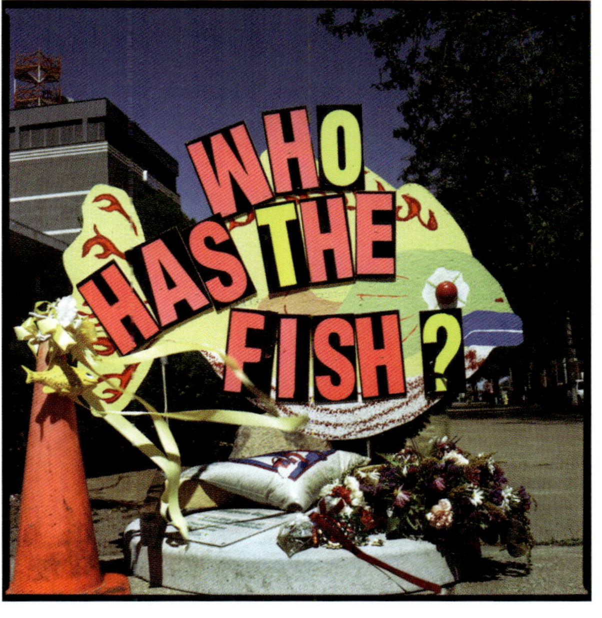

The Fish Commish broke the news to artist Chuck Benson, whose tongue-in-cheek response was, "I guess I should be complimented!"

And, then, like fried perch on the first Friday in Lent, like bikinis on Beach Six, like the lack of scales on whales, rumors were everywhere. Some of the most pervasive included:

1. The Fish Commish took it for publicity.
2. It was a fraternity prank.
3. Some out-of-town tourists took it to Canada, and it was for sale in a secondhand shop in Niagara Falls.
4. It's at the bottom of the bay.
5. The fire department stole it.
6. The "Coffeehouse Goths" took it.
7. Three young bald men in a Toyota 4-Runner filched it.
8. Two men, aged 20-25, carrying a mallet, took it and left in a small dark car.

The community rose up, shaking its metaphorical fist and demanding its fish be returned. Signs were posted at homes and businesses,* and countless letters to the editor appeared in the paper. The Sturgeon General was part of a public art project, but people took it *personally*.

As this book goes to print, the Sturgeon General is still at large. However, regardless of the outcome, we thank all the people who showed how much they care about GoFish!

* Joe and Tom Tssario, owners of West Lake Beer, had "Sturgeon General Call Home" up on their sign for weeks. They originally kidded about announcing "Sturgeon General Filets Cheap," but wanted to be sensitive to the issue. (However, if they were to recommend a beer to complement the Sturgeon, it would be "definitely an import— something light, yet heavy.")

oddsofrumor authenfishity

1. 1,000:1 Between press conferences, tons of media attention and speeches at the Rotary, Sertoma and Kiwanis Clubs, did we need more publicity?

2. 5:1 But stealing a fish is never as much fun as, say, singing Jimmy Buffett songs out the window all night long or shaving your behind.

3. 500:1 If someone was going to take a fish to Canada and sell it, Red, White & Bluegill would've gotten *a lot* more money.

4. 5,000:1 The fish are made of sealed fiberglass, people. They float.

5. 3,000:1 But they got the fish they wanted outside the station house already, remember?

6. 1,500:1 We don't know who these alleged people are, but imagine they're too busy drinking coffee, discussing philosophical matters and reading poetry—Things Typically Done At A Coffeehouse—to bother with a science/medicine-themed fish.

7. 25:1 This rumor is just elaborate enough to sound untrue.

8. 1,000,000:1 Unless it's the clown variety of small dark car. And ditto on #7.

Sturgeon General
artists: Chuck Benson & Jack Parks
patron: Lake Erie College of Osteopathic Medicine
location: West 10th & Sassafras Streets

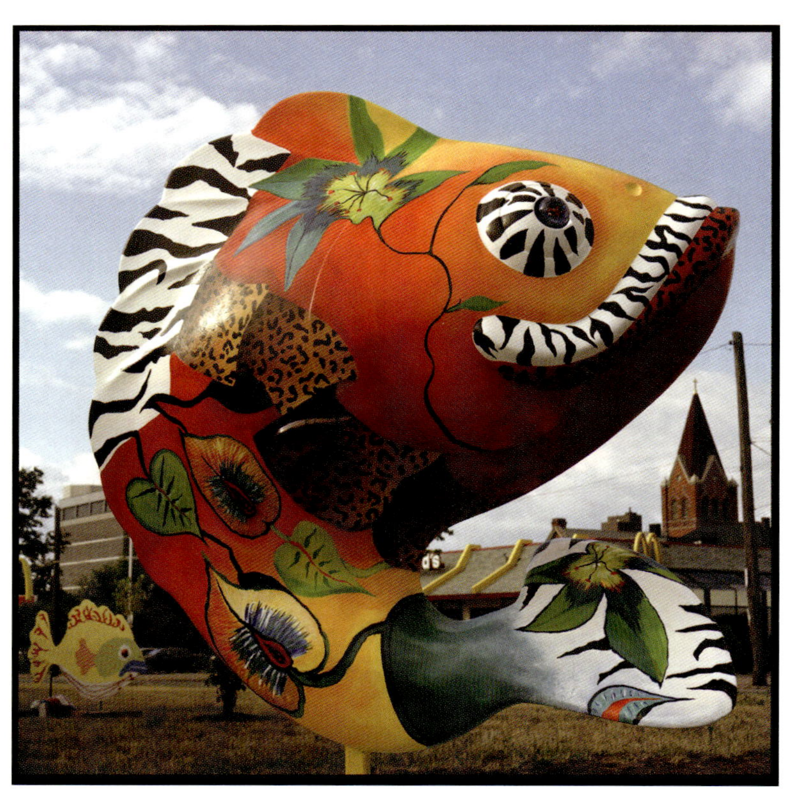

Beach House Fair
artists: Passle Helminski, Nickie Aziciri, Susan Stone
patron: Dr. Stanley Bogusz, Nikken Wellness Consultant, Erie/Warren, Pa.
location: West 12th & Sassafras Streets

mirandawarning

Dr. Stanley Bogusz had just a few specifications about the design of his fish, created by three female artist friends.

It was to be a nicely painted fish. It was not to be Carmen Miranda. And it was to match the décor of his beach house, where he planned to keep it on the back deck.

The artists visited the house so they could begin developing a design. It was done mostly in neutrals, but with splashes of strong color. They pulled those colors from the room in creating Beach House Fair, using the pillow hues for the flowers, a leopard stripe from the leopard rug, and hot reds from a red wall in the kitchen. The fish was designed to reflect the furnishings of the house.

Dr. Bogusz plans hold an unveiling celebration when the fish is relocated to the deck, and all three artists hope to attend.

what goes around, comes around

"I spent fifteen years living in Erie, meeting and marrying my wife, Amy, before moving to Lehigh Valley in 1999. But this summer, we returned to Erie to visit friends. While eating lunch at a restaurant at the dock, we saw one of the fish and found out about the GoFish! project. From the restaurant, we proceeded to the Library gift shop, where we found the fish sponsored by Plaza Dental, where Amy worked for more than half her years in Erie. As she began to reminisce about Plaza Dental, we realized that the fish was a sign that we should drop in at Plaza Dental later that day. Amy hadn't visited her friends and colleagues there since we'd left Erie. Later that afternoon, we did stop in and boy, were we glad we did. Amy had the best time seeing folks and catching up with what everyone had been doing these past two years. The afternoon we spent at Plaza Dental was a highlight of our visit to Erie, and we owe it all to a fish!"

Carl Mann

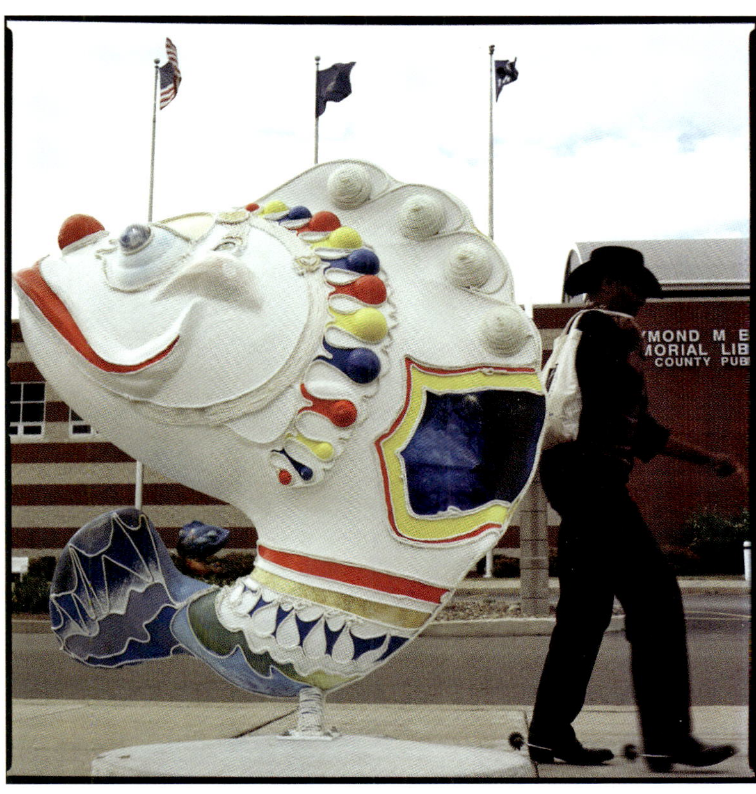

Carousel Race
artist: Clement C. Buseck
patron: Plaza Dental Associates
location: 160 East Front Street

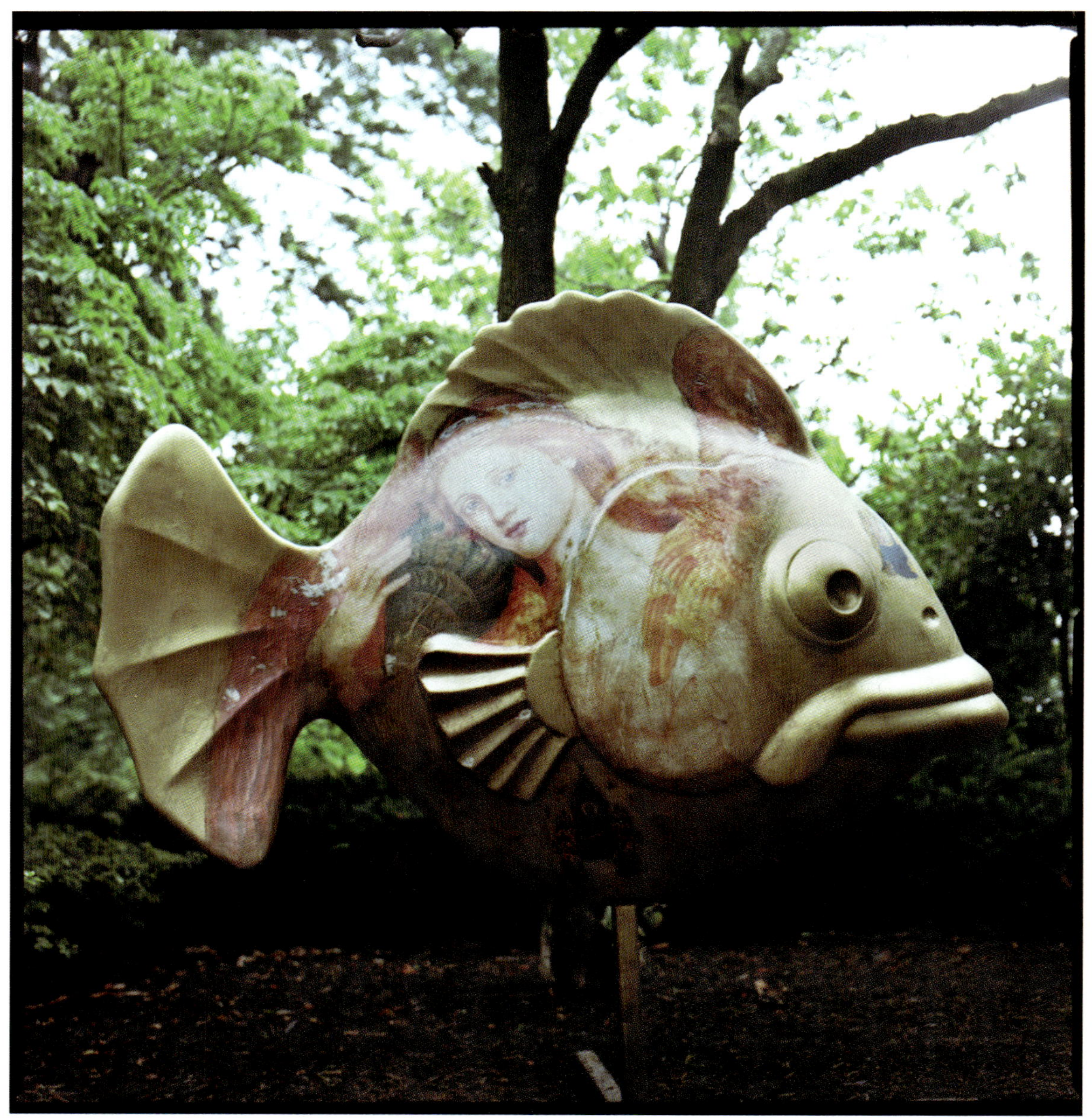

Angelic Fish
artists: Louis Christian Caravaglia and Jean Craige Pepper
patron: The Philadelphia Trust Company
location: West 10th & Sassafras Streets

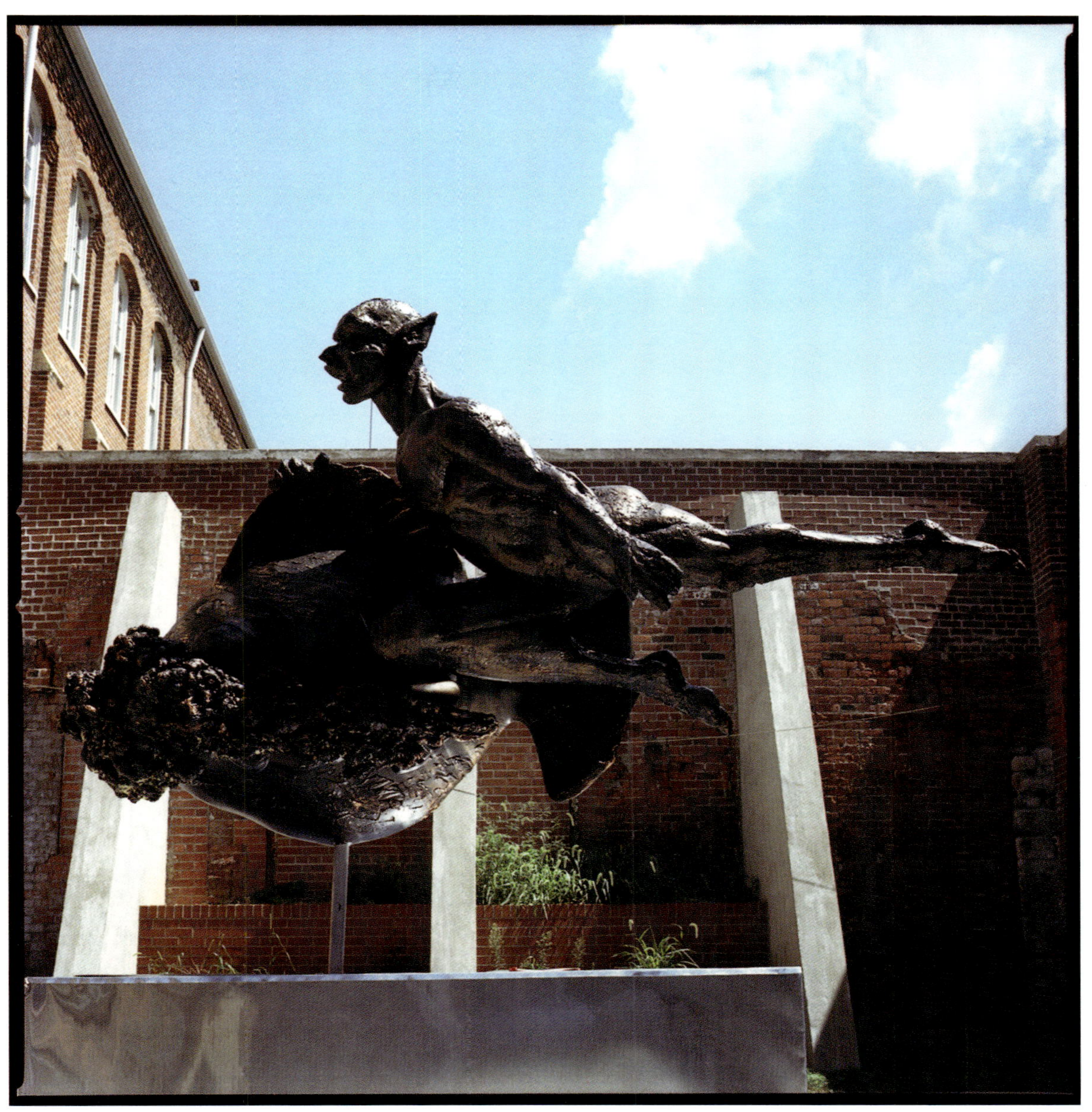

Full Fathom Five
artist: John Edwards
patron: donated to the Erie Team PA CareerLink by the Greater Erie Economic Development Corporation
location: East 14th & French Streets (in the courtyard)

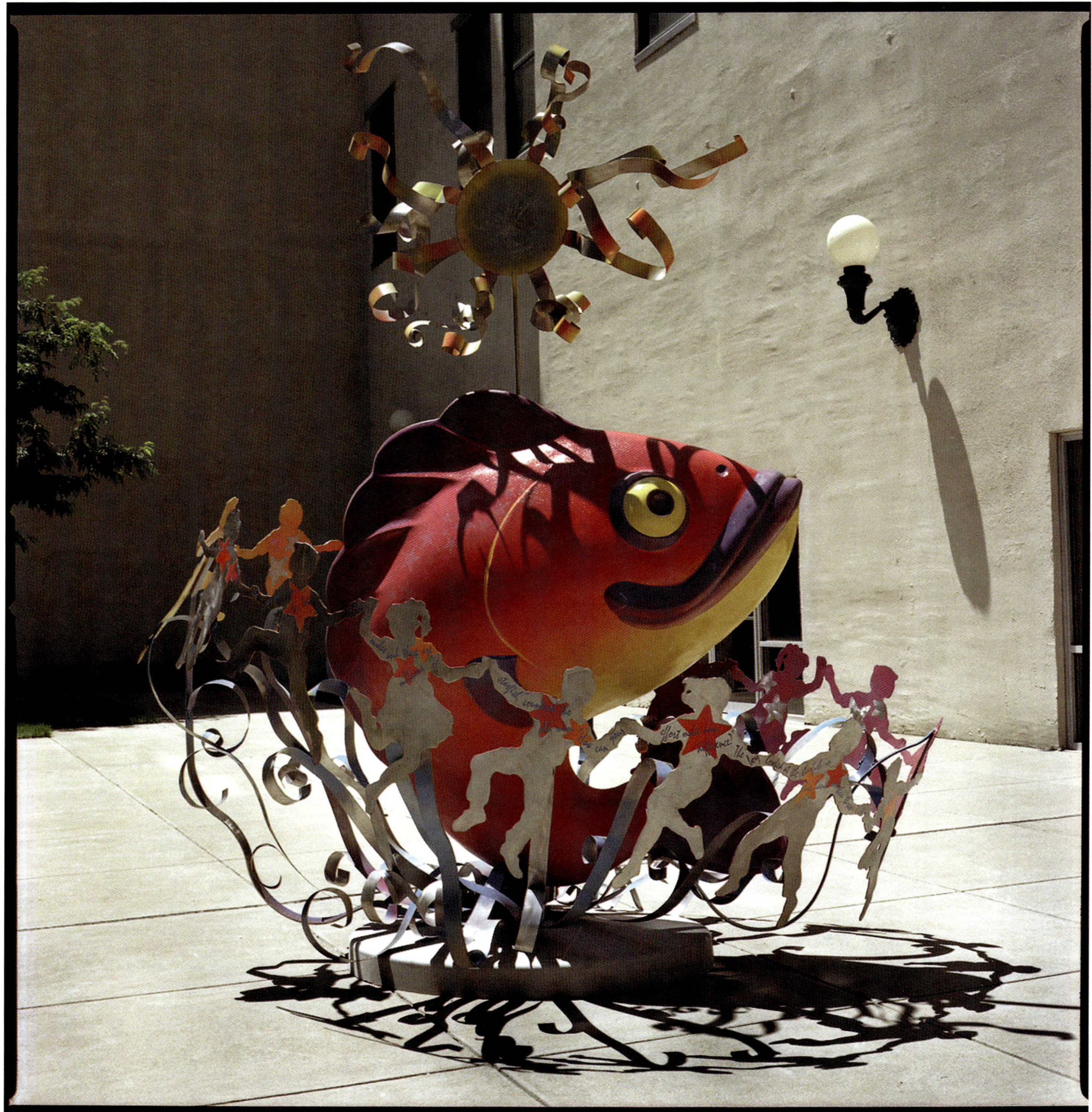

agroupereffort

Frank DiPlacido, who created a GoFish! fish for the Sarah Reed Children's Center, needed to mix auto body paint for the project and didn't know how to do it.

Good thing the kids could teach him.

Frank works at the Erie County Technical School through a partnership with Sarah Reed Children's Center, supervising their alternative education program. He tried to involve the kids as much as possible in creating the fish, which is based upon the Sarah Reed logo. They were cutting out the metal shapes, doing the welds, and even training him on how to mix the auto body paint.

In addition to the help provided by his students, Frank had lots of donations for which he was thankful—The Warren Company donated steel, Lakeshore Markers donated the stencils, Millcreek Parks & Recreation helped with transportation, and the other teachers pitched in to help, too.

And the kids at the Technical School were so excited, some even helped out over their vacation time.

"This is the neatest thing. I saw this link in the Memphis, Tenn. newspaper, and when I accessed it, I was delighted to see what you are doing as a city project. More cities should have a similar project. It brings a smile to one's face, and, let's face it, we need to smile."

Charlotte Wolfe

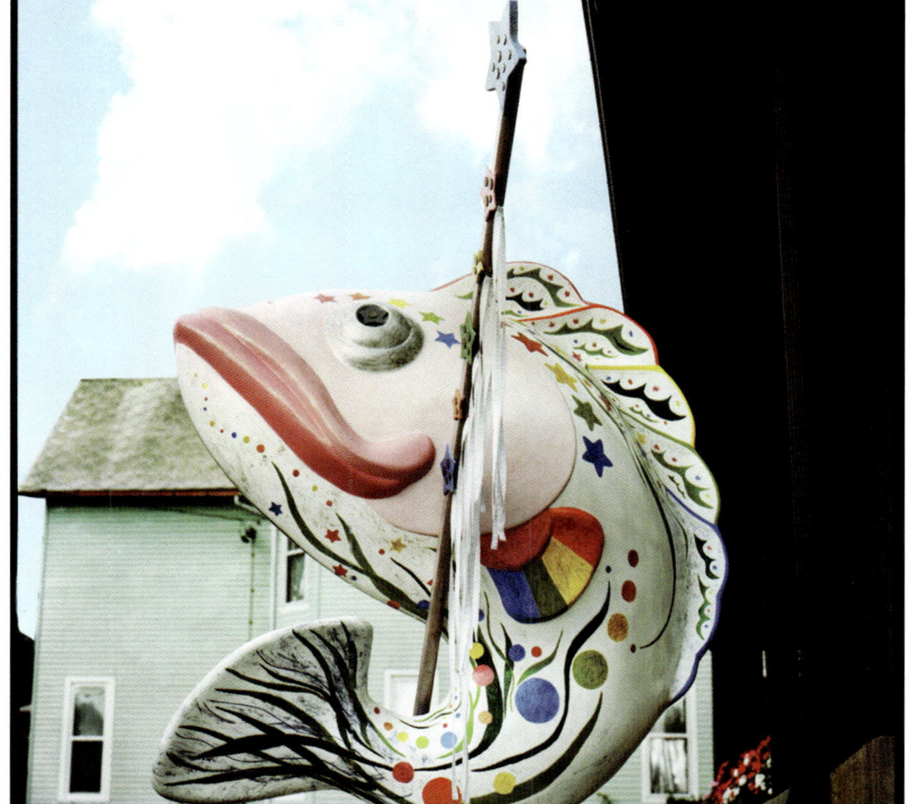

A Child's Fish Tale: Sarah Reed Children's Center
artist: Frank DiPlacido, assisted by E.C.T.S.
patron: Howard Industries
location: 8th & State Streets
Life Lesson Award
Teaches a lesson or brings an awareness

Dantia
artist: Monica Schwegman
patron: Dr. Greg Garcia
location: 3219 Peach Street

howhighcanyoucount?

For the record: Dan Burke is an artist, not a mathematician.

Which is why, although the fish he created represents a visual illustration of how many people are in Erie county based upon the 2000 census, there is not a single numeral to be found anywhere on it.

Dan began by dividing the fish into equal sections, with four quadrants per side. Then he started making hash marks.

In the Native Hawaiian or other Pacific Islander section, he made 61. For American Indian or Alaskan Native, he did 464. Under Asian, he illustrated 1929. For Two or more races, he slashed 3499 times. For Black or African-American, Dan created 17,202 marks. And for White, he fashioned 255,282 notches.

That's right. Two hundred fifty-five thousand, two hundred and eighty-two. According to Dan, that's an average of 430 hash marks per square inch.

Go ahead and count 'em, if you like!

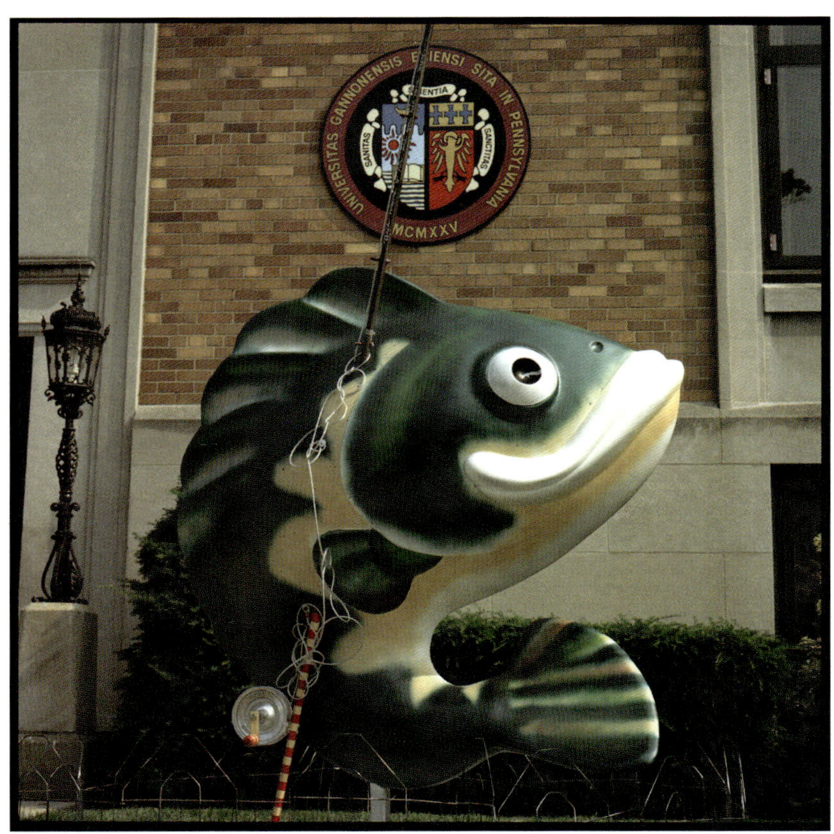

"The Teaching Fish" Minds to Learn, Fins to Serve
artist: MC Gensheimer
patrons: The Chaplain's Office, Campus Ministry and The Center for Social Concerns, Gannon University
location: 109 West 6th Street

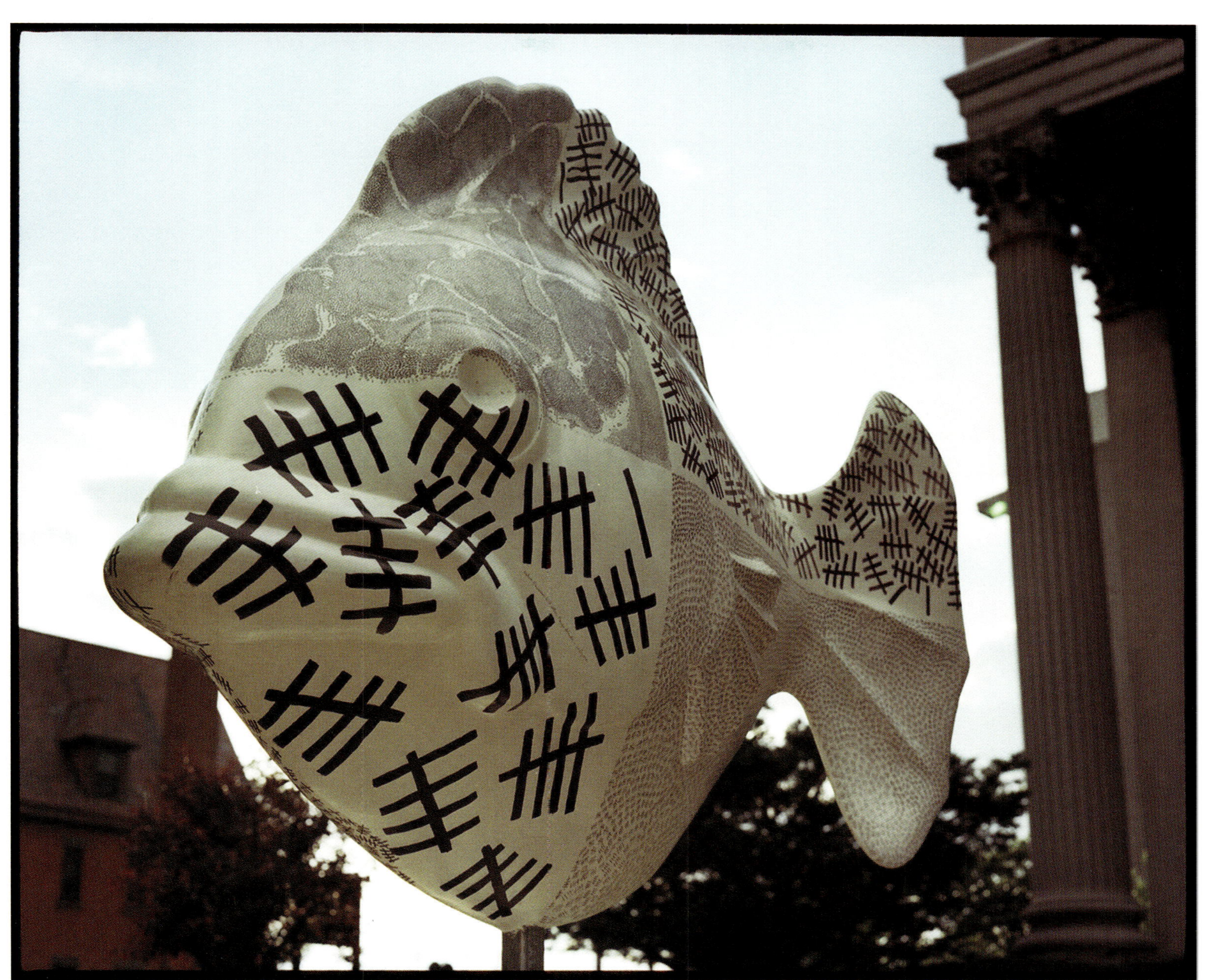

280,843 Fish
artist: Daniel Burke
patron: Erie County
location: 140 West 6th Street

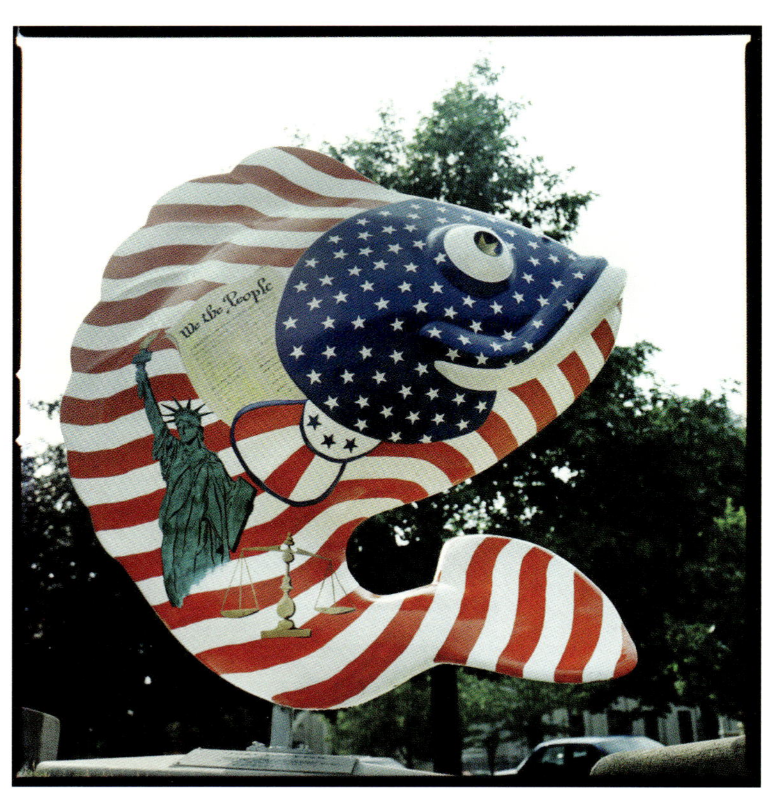

Just-us Fish
artist: Kate Arkwright
patron: Elderkin, Martin, Kelly & Messina
location: West 6th & Peach Streets

scalesofjustice

Kate Arkwright was pleased to be creating a fish for a local law firm. Even more so one day when she heard a pounding on her front door and opened it to find two policemen. Apparently, someone had seen the fish in her garage, where she worked on it late at night, and called to report that she'd stolen it.

Luckily, Kate's explanation that she was an artist, and an invitation to call the law firm sponsoring the fish got her off the, uh, hook.

(Note: A photograph of this fish will be on display at the Historical Society of Pennsylvania, from Sept. 2001-April 2002. It is included in an exhibit called Liberty on the Anvil, 1701-2001: Exploring the Legacies of Pennsylvania's Founding Charters. In this exhibit, they are displaying the range of uses to which Americans have put the image of the Liberty Bell over the years.)

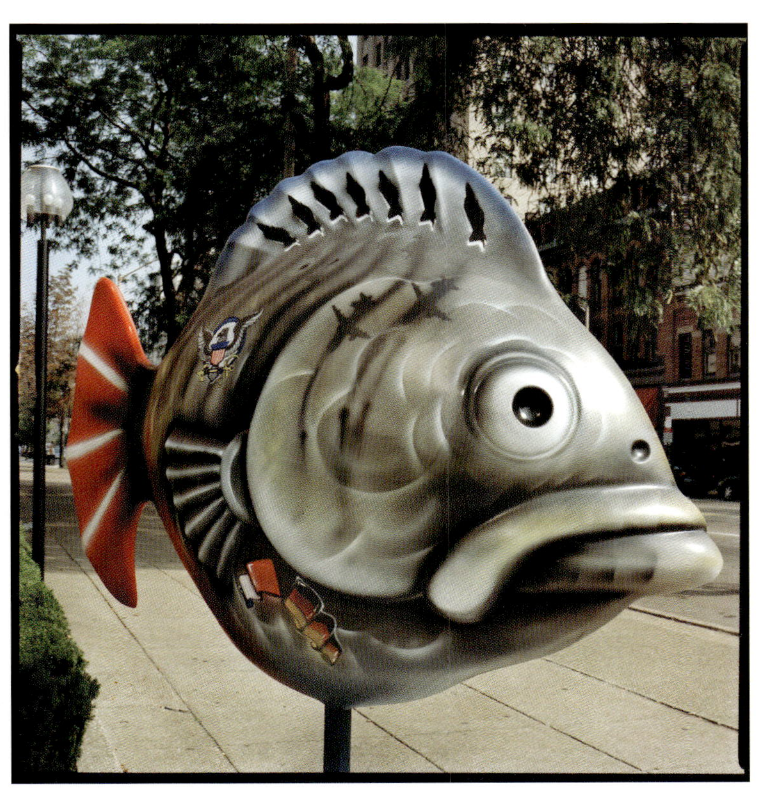

Hooked on Flying: Semper Fi(sh)
artist: Eddie Portillo
patrons: Erie Aviation, Inc.,
Conner Holding Company
location: 11th & State Streets

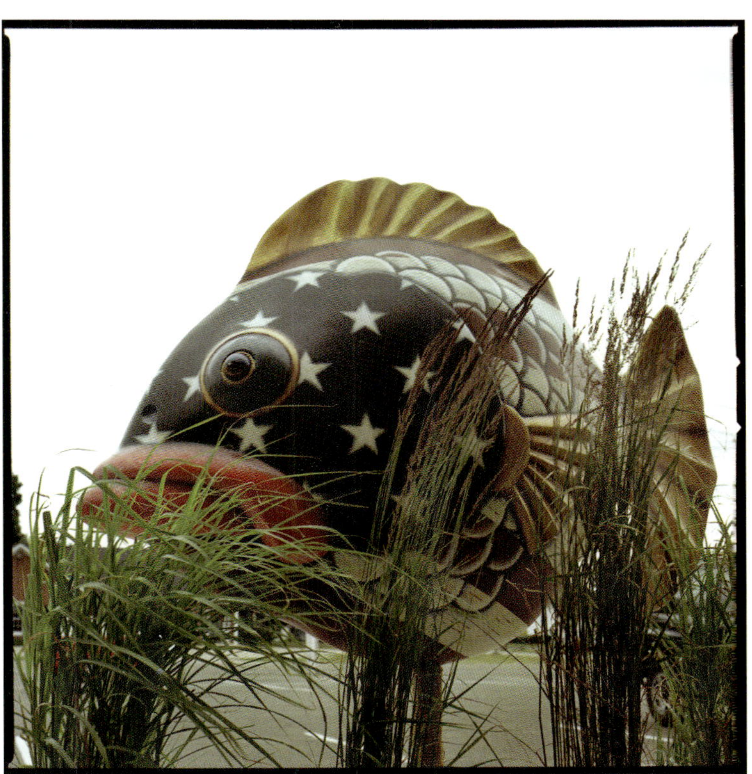

Oh Say Can You Sea
artist: Betsy Riehl
patrons: Rustic & Refined, Riehl Gardens
location: 2592 West 8th Street

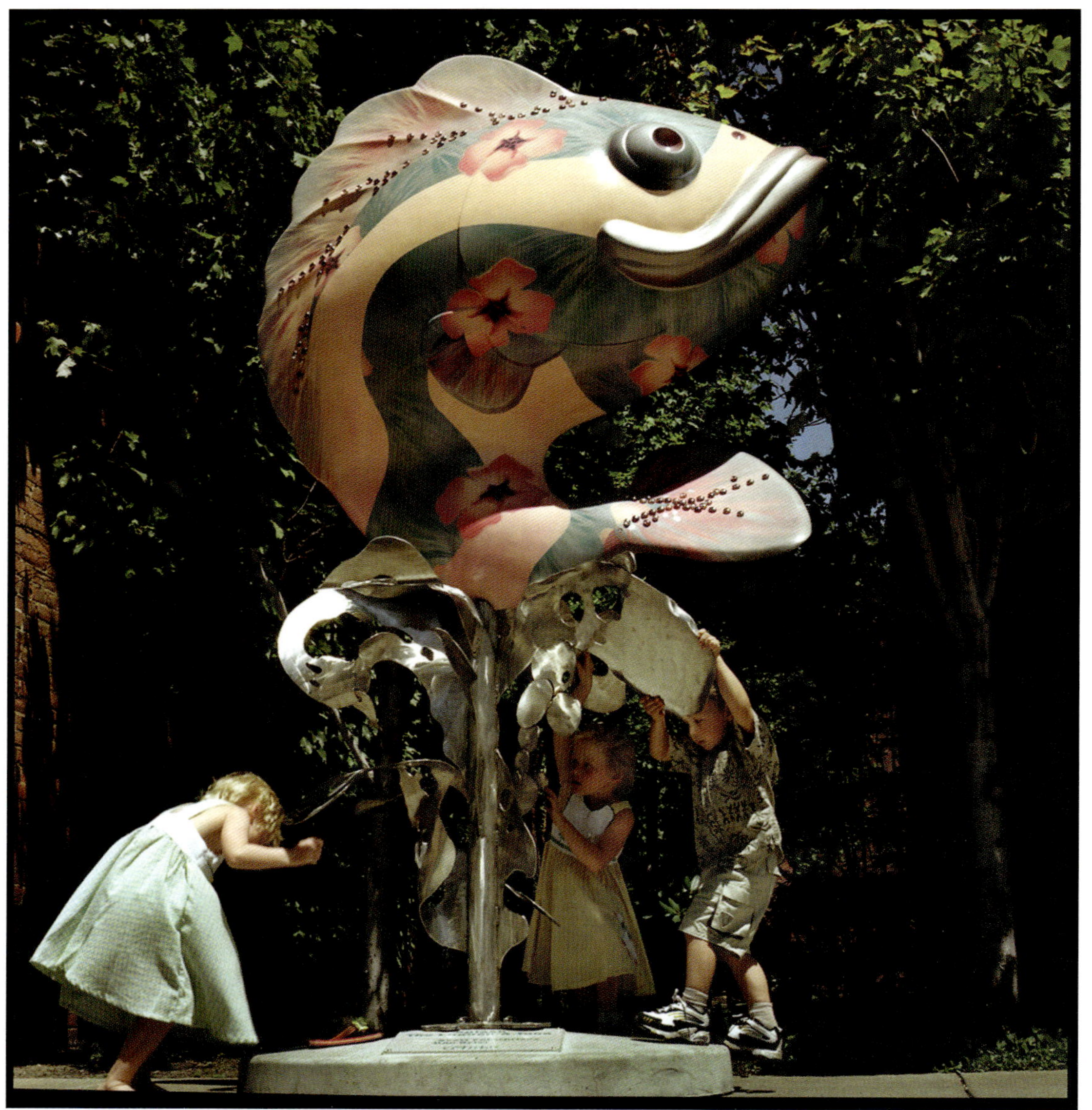

Splash-the-Lagoon-A-Tuna
artist: Dan Byler
patron: Scott Enterprises
location: 815 State Street

welcometo motherhood,dan

According to artist Dan Byler, producing this fish was like giving birth. It was like going through all the labor, and then heaving a great sigh.

His original thought was to work within a musical theme, as sponsor Nick Scott is both an accomplished pianist and an active supporter of the Erie Philharmonic. He was thinking scales. Tune-a. Fins as black and white keyboard keys. But, somewhere along the way, musical gave way to tropical, and the final product became a fish with salmon and purple stripes with big hibiscus flowers (though the artist is quick to emphasize that he made sure it didn't look like a tablecloth).

Working on it in his studio, the doors of which hadn't been opened in 20 years, Dan fielded visits from his Frontier area neighbors, who stopped by every morning to see how it was going, and children from a nearby home daycare, who walked over en masse each day to check his progress. He also made new friends along the way— fellow artist Evan Everhart, who helped him with the base, and the fine folks at Valu Home Center, where he made many, many trips for spraypaint.

ourfishwasmissed

"HeART and Sole suffered damage from unknown 'aliens.' The fish was stripped of its epoxy and it rotated on its pole support. When the Offishial Hosfishal Nurses and Doctors arrived, alas, the fish was sicker than expected.

HeART had been broken and split and needed to be taken back to the studio. The space in front of the Art House was empty. The Art House children asked, 'Where's our fish?' We had many people come to our door to inquire on the whereabouts of the fish. They were disappointed and yes disheartened to find out that the fish had been vandalized.

After 14 days away HeArt received new Sole. She was repaired, repainted and reinstalled. As HeART and Sole was placed in her righful environment again, we heard clapping and cheers from the neighbors across the street. 'We're so glad it's back—we missed it.'

I've had several people pass by, stop and comment, 'We're so glad and lucky to have a fish in our neighborhood. Thank you.'"

Sr. Margaret Ann Pilewski, OSB

HeART & Sole

artists: Neighborhood Art House Children, Patty Czulewicz and Sister Margaret Ann Pilewski

patron: National City Bank

location: 201 East 10th Street

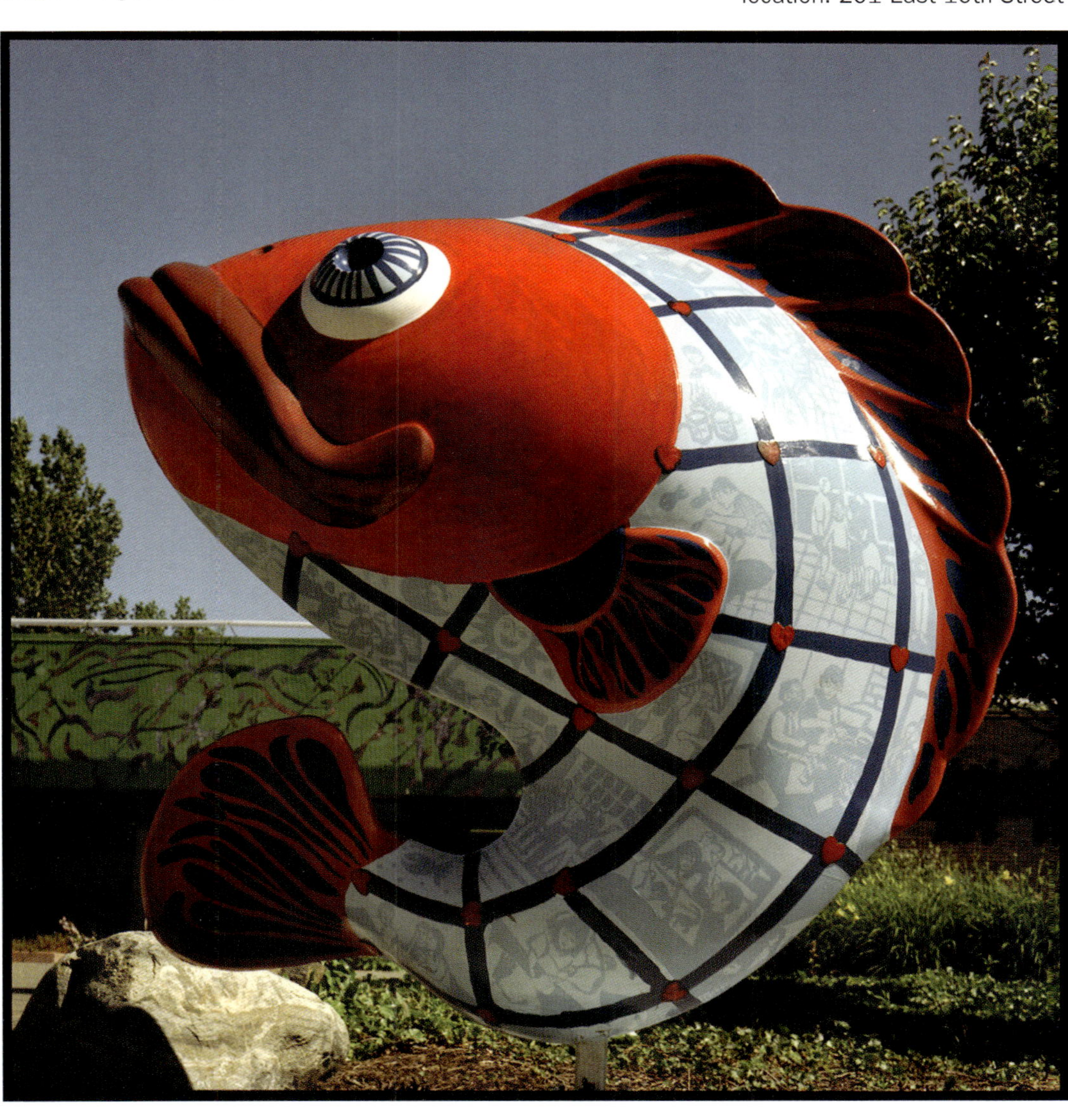

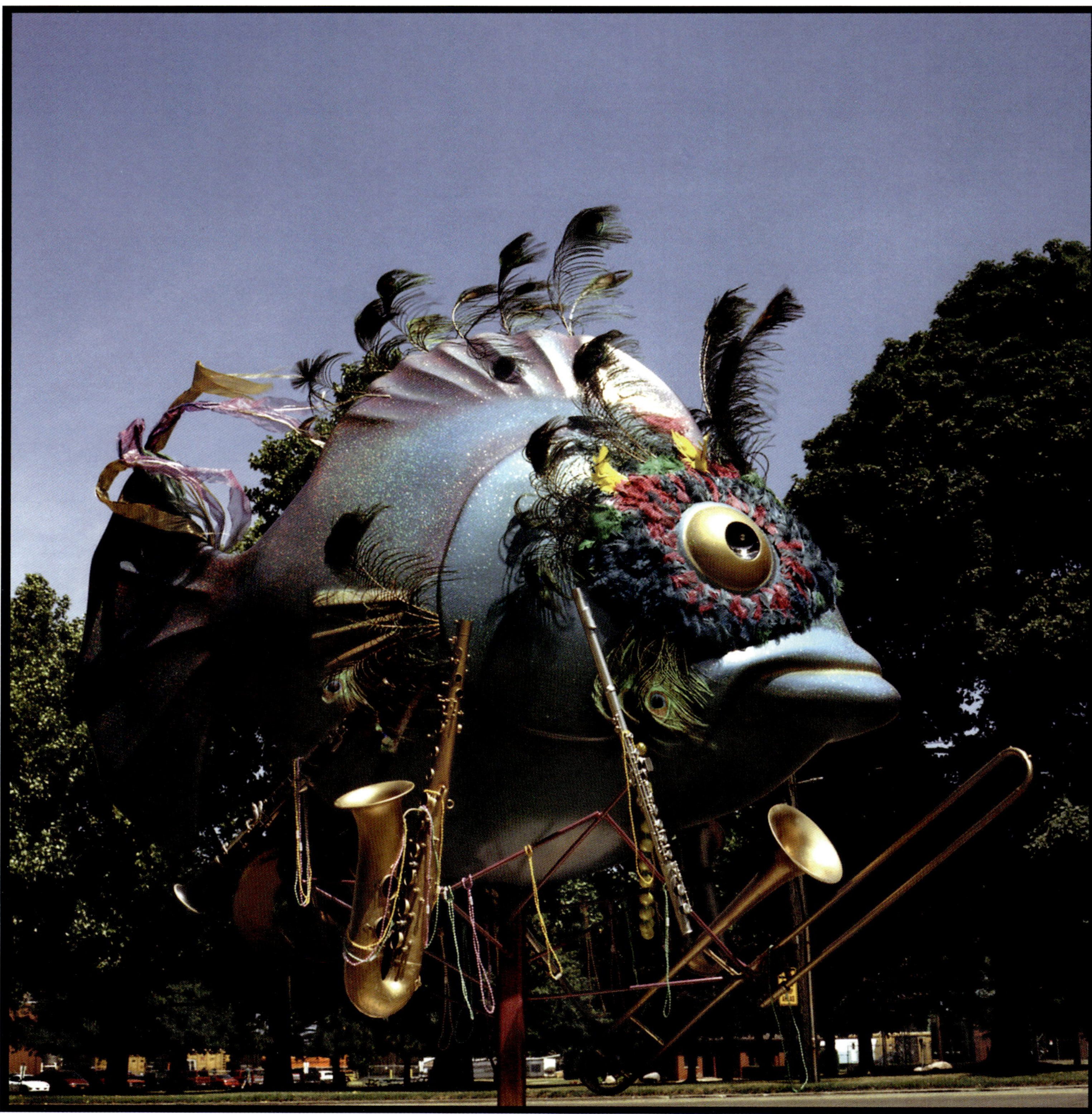

billandfred's excellentadventure

Thirteen years ago, Bill Doan, Gannon's Dean of the College of Humanities, Business and Education, met Frederick Franck while directing one of his plays and a friendship began. Frederick was born in Holland in 1909. In the span of his 92 years, he has been an oral surgeon, serving on the staff of Albert Schweitzer in the African jungle, was the only artist to draw the entire proceedings of Vatican II, and has written more than thirty books. His drawings, paintings, and sculptures are part of the permanent collections of museums around the world, including the Museum of Modern Art in New York City.

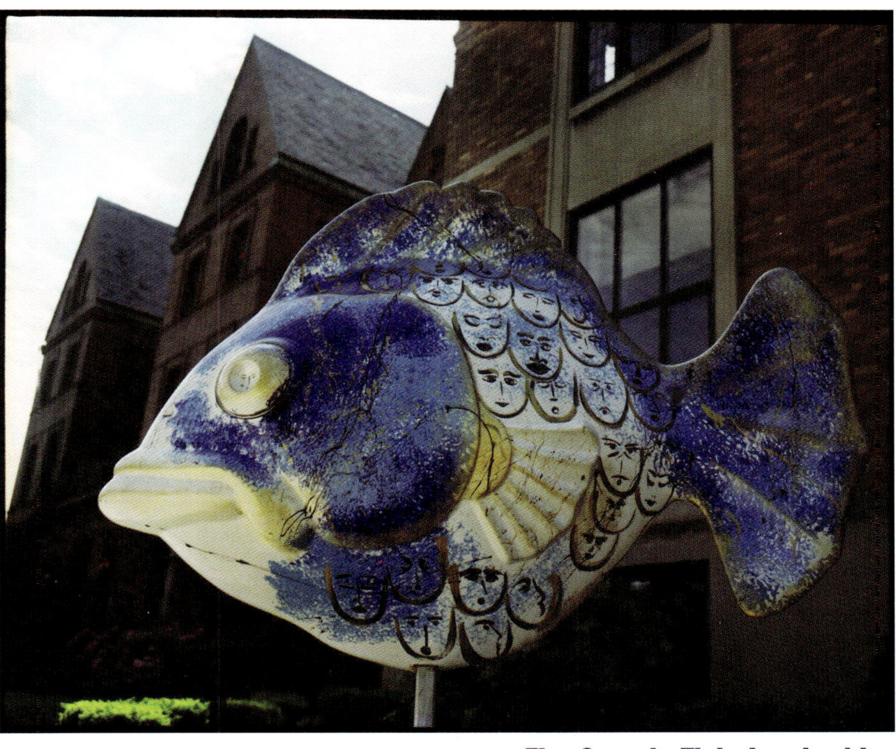

The Cosmic Fish, Inspired by Frederick Franck
artist: William J. Doan
patron: Gannon University
location: 109 West 6th Street

Bill is currently at work on two projects with Frederick. One is a biographical work that examines Frederick's work in the context of twentieth century art and spirituality, and the other is an edited collection of newsletters, called The Shoestring, that Frederick has produced for the last thirty-three years.

About the projects, he says, "I have been interviewing Frederick over the past four months, recording our conversations and transcribing the tapes for use in the book. I consider myself very fortunate to have developed a personal relationship with Frederick. His life has spanned the entire twentieth century. As a child, he stood in his front yard and watched the Kaiser's army march across Holland in WWI, witnessed first hand the death and destruction of WWII, and has never given in to a sense of hopelessness or despair. To this day, he believes that 'Art is that, which despite all, gives hope.'"

The Cosmic Fish was inspired by Frederick Franck's painting of the same name, the original of which hangs in the Tokyo National Museum, Tokyo, Japan.

les fishtivities du Mardi Gras
artists: Elisa Guida, Ed Saloum, Jay & Darby Scalise
patron: donated to the GECAC Community Charter School by The Greater Erie Economic Development Corporation
location: 1450 East Lake Road

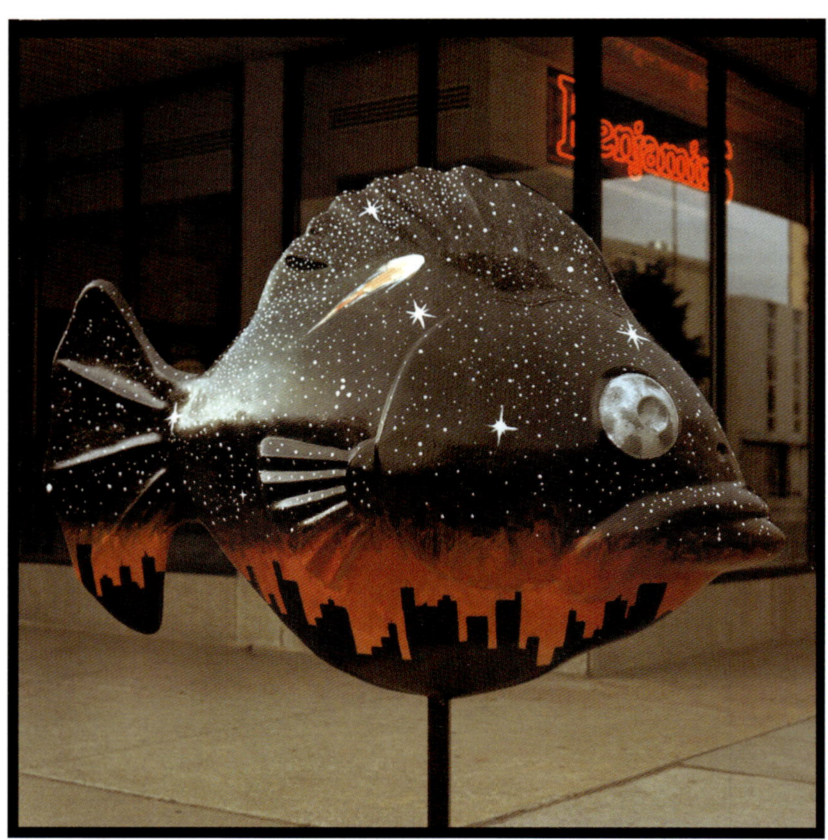

Sushi Sunset, over Cosmic Tuna
artist: Nick Royer
patron: Lamar Outdoor Advertising
location: West 10th & Peach Streets

cosmictunahandroll withsushisunsetsauce

by Chef Patrick Rodgers of Crowley's Restaurant

1 Nori wrapper
2 oz. Cosmic Tuna (raw)
1/4 oz. wasabi (Japanese horseradish)
1 oz. garlic aioli (homemade garlic mayonnaise)
1/4 oz. diakon root
1/2 bunch diakon sprouts
1/4 cup sushi rice
1/4 cup sliced avocado

Fill Nori wrapper with thinly sliced tuna. Spread wasabi and aioli over tuna. Top with sushi rice and julienned diakon root. Roll nori into a cone shape. Top with sliced avocado and diakon sprouts. Drizzle with Sushi Sunset Sauce.

Sushi Sunset Sauce

1/2 cup teriyaki marinade
1 tsp. sesame oil
1/4 cup rice wine vinegar
1 T. honey
1 t. Siracha hot sauce

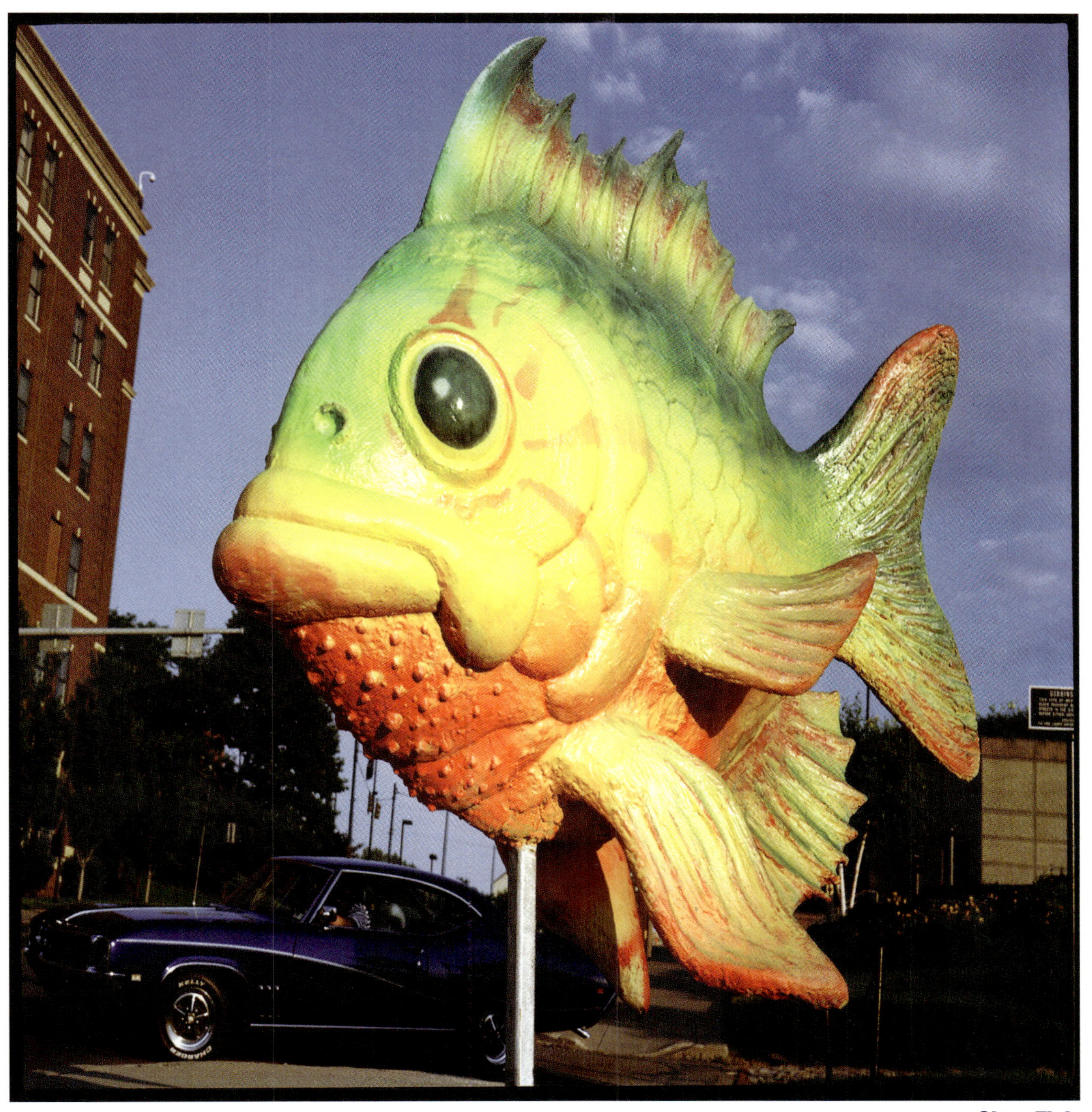

Glow Fish
artist: Paul Frazer
patron: First Energy
location: 100 State Street

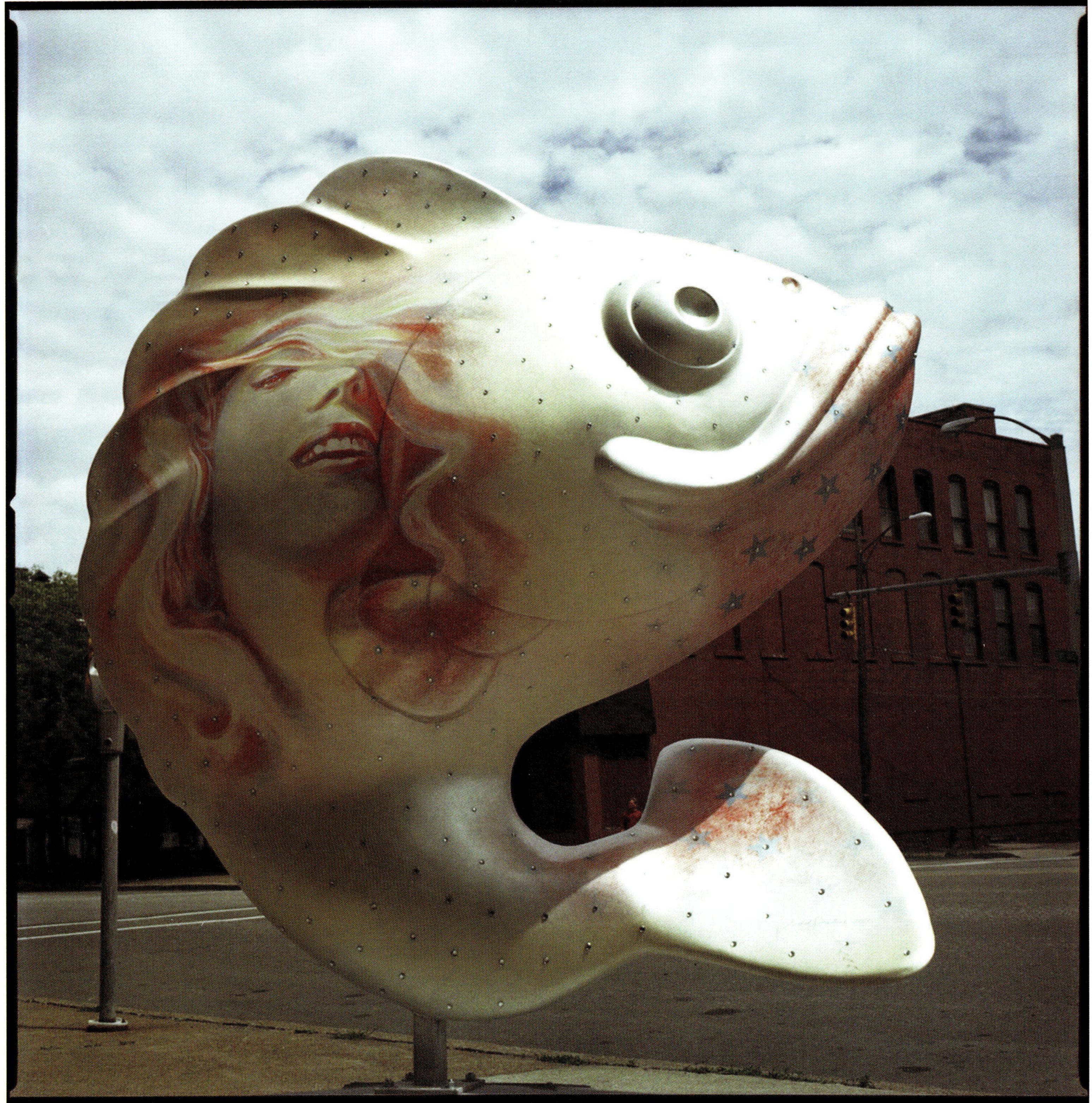

“Downtown Erie is not the only place awash with brightly colored fish...”

“Festive denizens of the deep, carefully crafted by the patients at the Shriners Hospitals for Children, Erie, decorated the hospital’s corridors during national Child Life Week (July 9-13).

Inspired by Erie’s GoFish! project, Shriners Hospital developed its own GoFiSHC (Shriners Hospitals for Children) program as a way to celebrate Child Life Week, a national celebration to highlight child life services and programs at hospitals throughout the country.

Each of the 10 fish “sculptures” at the hospital included an informative paragraph about Child Life services. The Child Life staff at Shriners Hospital got employees involved in the GoFiSCH project by creating a game using the fish. Employees won prizes by visiting each hospital fish and matching the name of the fish with its informative paragraph.

The Shriners Hospital GoFiSCH project was a big hit with everyone involved. While the hospital was unable to secure a GoFish! of its own to display for the enjoyment of the children, this project helped carry on the spirit of the community effort.”

Bob Howden

Bluefish
artist: Mark Weber
patron: Highmark Blue Cross Blue Shield
location: 8th & State Streets

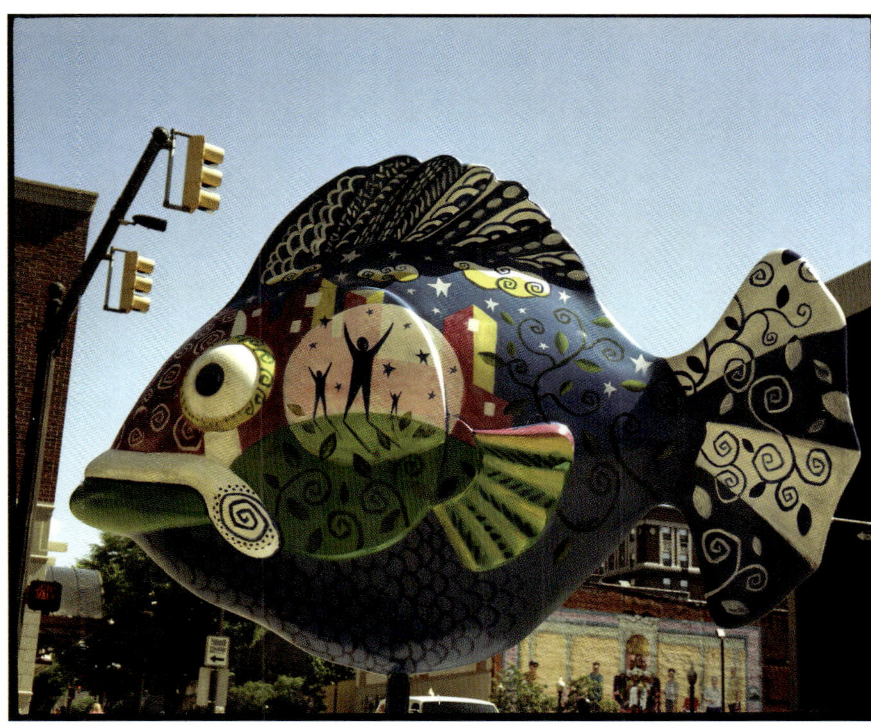

SuperStarFish
artist: Todd Scalise
patron: Sea Cave–Erie’s Aquarium Store
location: 1402 State Street

mypersonaltrainer,mr.fish

Susan Miller, compliance officer/regulatory survey coordinator for Hamot Health Center, not only coordinates fish walks for a group of co-workers, she's arranged her entire exercise routine around walking from fish to fish. And with good reason— Susan has been training to do a 60-mile, 3-day benefit walk as a tribute to her mother, a breast cancer survivor. Although work-related obligations will keep her from participating this October as originally intended, she's glad to have had the benefit of training and hopes to complete the walk next year. Susan credits the fish for having helped her with her commitment to exercise.

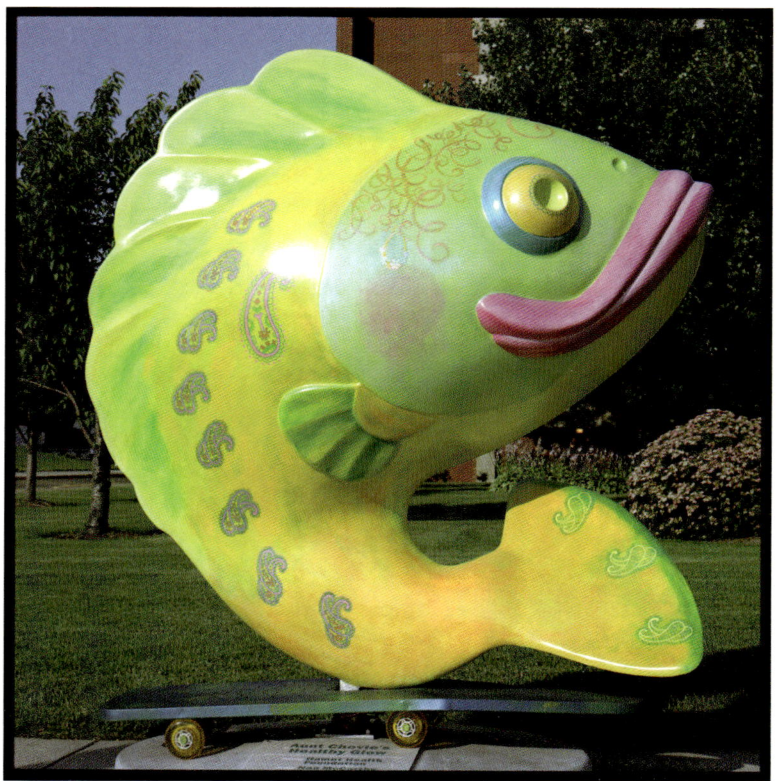

Aunt Chovie's Healthy Glow
artist: Nan McCarthy Salvatore
patron: Hamot Health Foundation
location: 201 State Street

Hooked on Braces
artist: Sandy Fernando
patron: Dr. Jack Utley's Orthodontic Team
location: 3900 Zuck Road

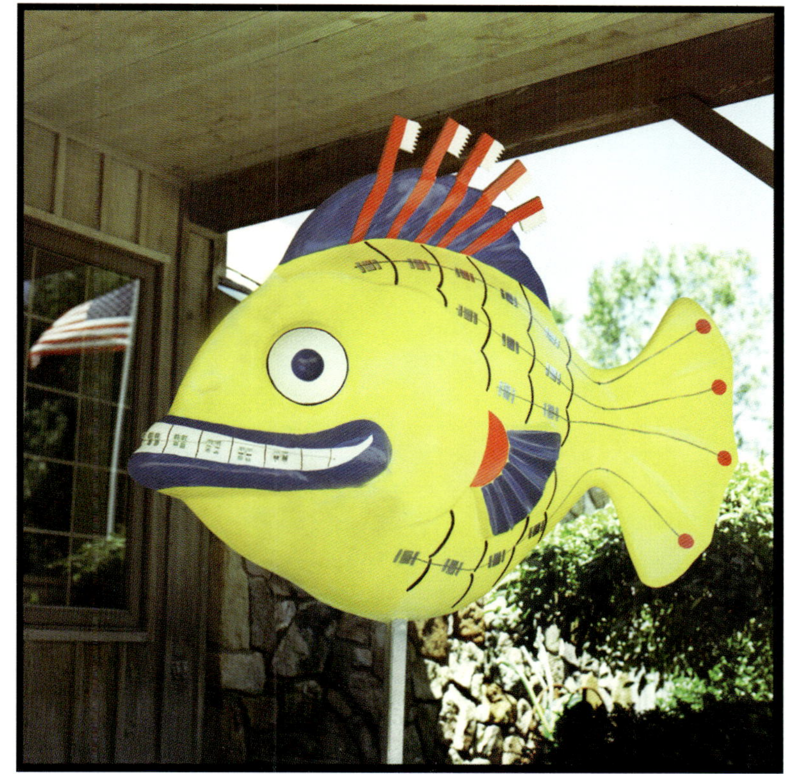

workingtooth-gether

Soon after Dr. Utley bought a fish, he bumped into the mother of Sandy Fernando, a former patient. He learned that Sandy was heading off to medical school, but at Brown University, she had majored in art.

The metaphorical lightbulb went off in Dr. Utley's head, shining as brightly as a set of silvery braces. Might she be interested in doing his fish? It turned out that she might— in fact, she was in his office to discuss it within the half-hour.

Dr. Utley's direction was this: "I want a toy fish! A happy fish! Volkswagen yellow!" And thus, Hooked on Braces was born. The fish, however, has now been rechristened "Chinook on Zuck"— congratulations to Meagan Cousins, winner of the office's naming contest.

fishbonding

"I thought that seeing all of the fish with my little sister from Family Services' Big Brothers/Big Sisters would be a fun idea. Boy, was it. I'm not sure who has enjoyed it more, her or me.

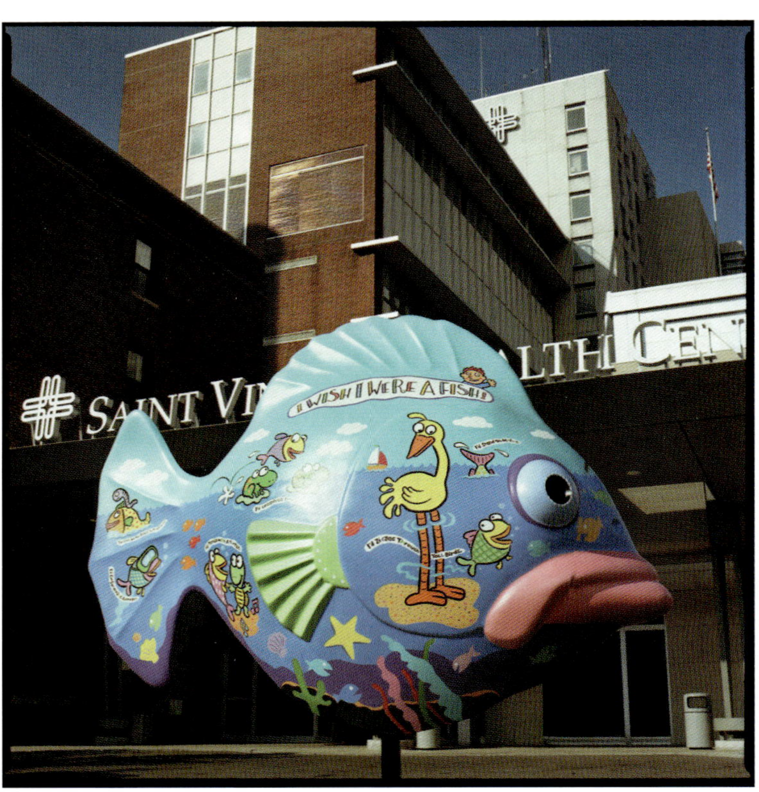

Fish Wish
artist: Tom Tucker
patron: Saint Vincent Health Center
location: 232 West 25th Street

We have been driving around town for weeks taking pictures with all of the fish. We have been mocking them in their personalities and have been laughing ever since. My little sister is a shy individual and this had definitely broken her out of her shell. I've never seen her so happy, and thrilled to do something in the year and a half that I have known her. She calls me to let me know about the new ones that she has seen, and wants me to come over right away to get her picture with them. She has not only had fun talking to me about it but has told all of her friends and everyone that she has come in contact with. When we are out and other people are doing the same thing, she will blurt out, 'we've already got pictures with 63 of them,' and so on from there.

Looking at all those fish takes quite an appetite on us after a day of GoFishing on a Sunday afternoon. So we usually close the day with lunch and talk about all of the fishes that we have seen for the day."

Lela Checco

Puzzle Pisces
artists: Dr. Gertrude A. Barber Center Participants & Staff
patron: Marquette Savings Bank
location: 3rd & East Avenue

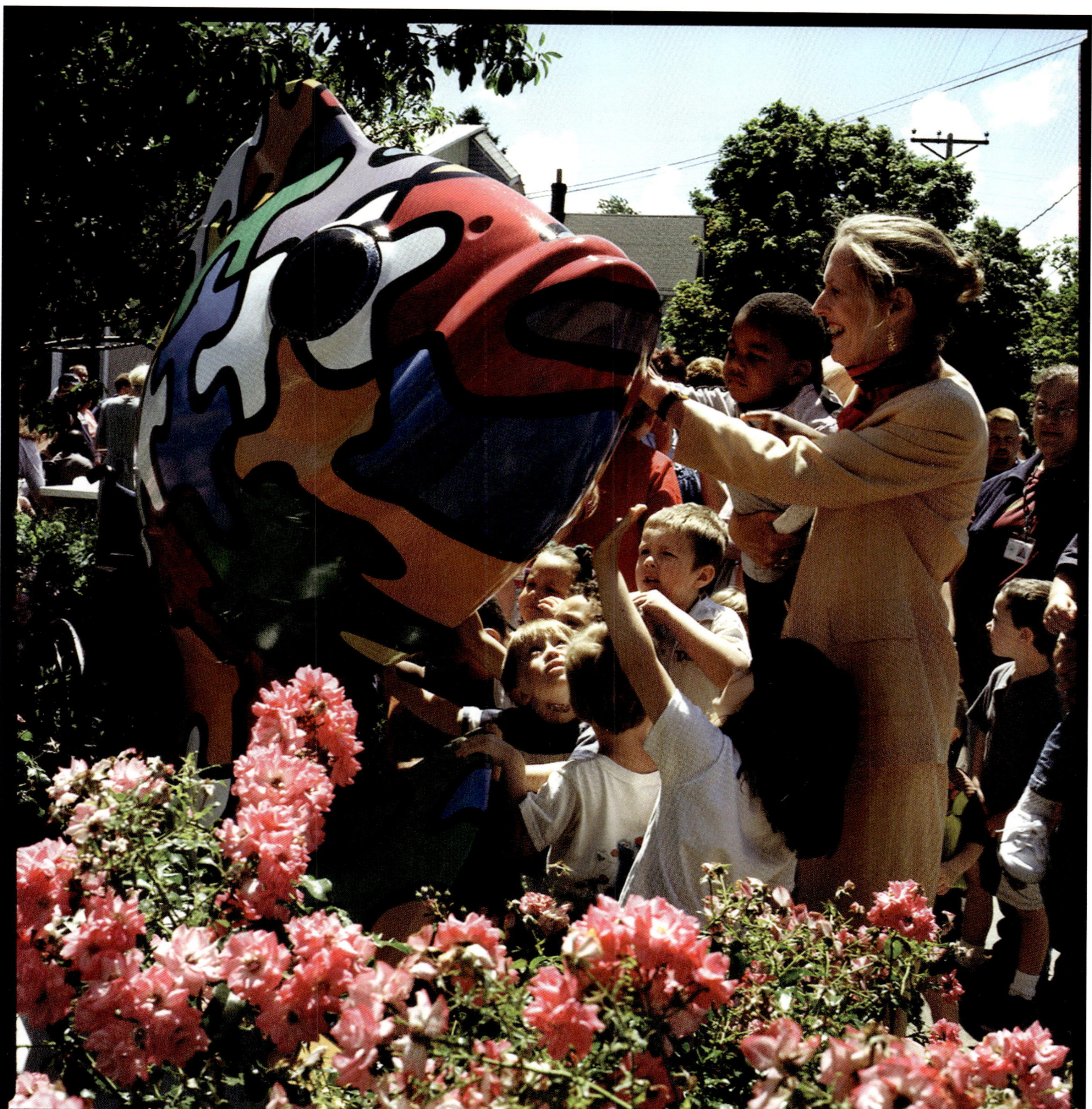

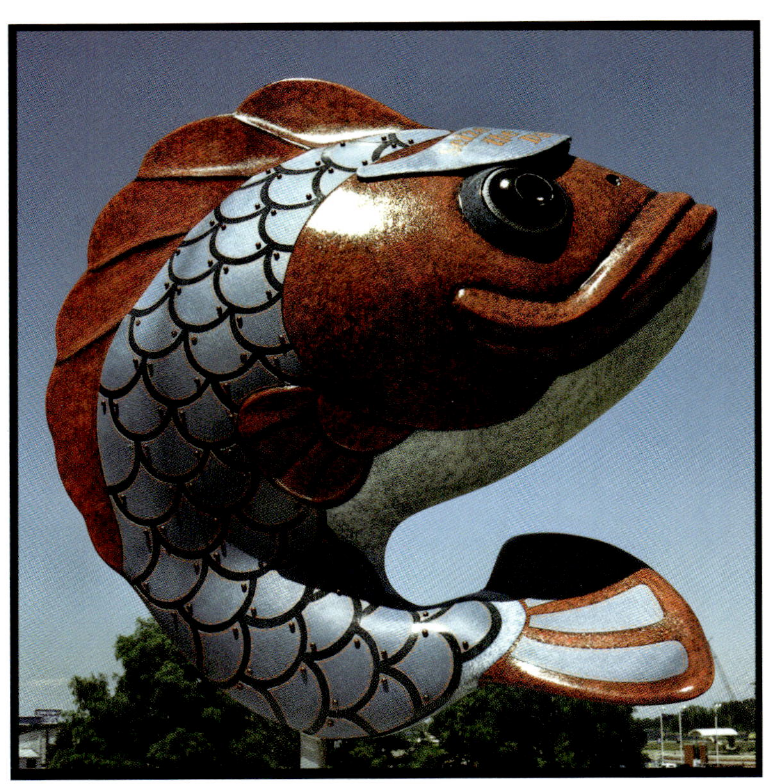

Carpe Denim
artist: Frank Fecko
patron: GE Transportation Systems
location: State Street & Bayfront Highway

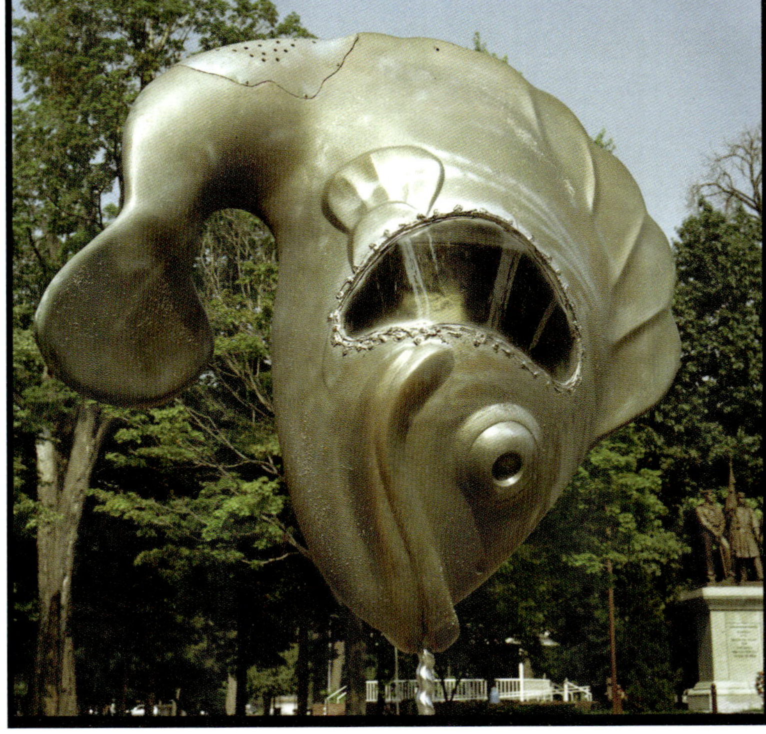

Fish Eye
artist: Steven Kemenyffy
patron: PHB
location: West 6th & Peach Streets

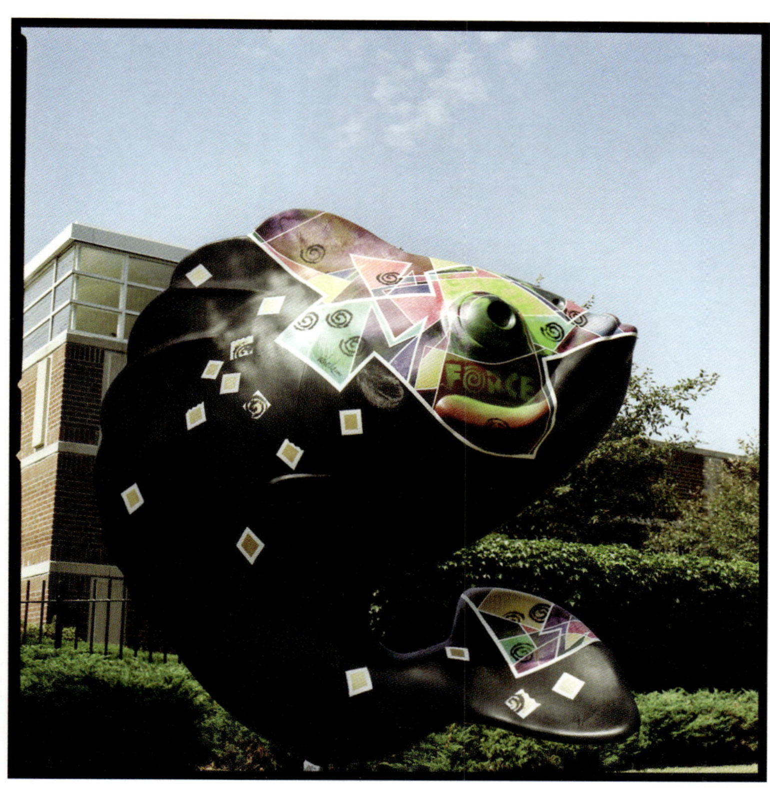

Glinodo Earth Force: Healthy Habitats Forever
artists: Doug & Penny Irish-Hosler
patron: Pennsylvania Center for Travel, Tourism & Film
location: East 6th & Holland Streets

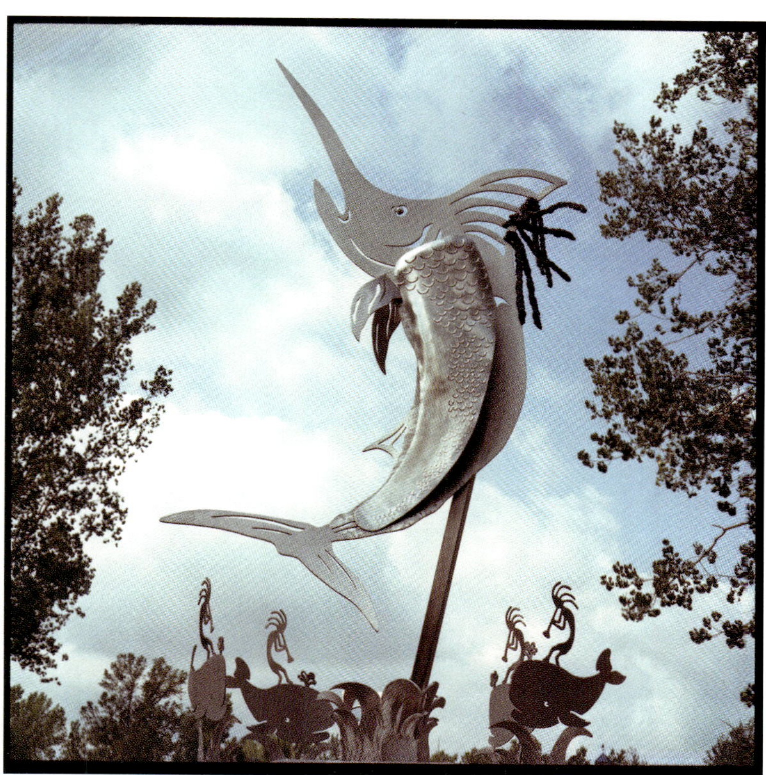

Bob Marlin & the Whalers
artists: Wayne Cunningham, Jim Rutkowski, Jr. & Charlie Rutkowski
patron: Industrial Sales & Manufacturing, Inc.
location: Sara's Campground & Restaurant, Presque Isle

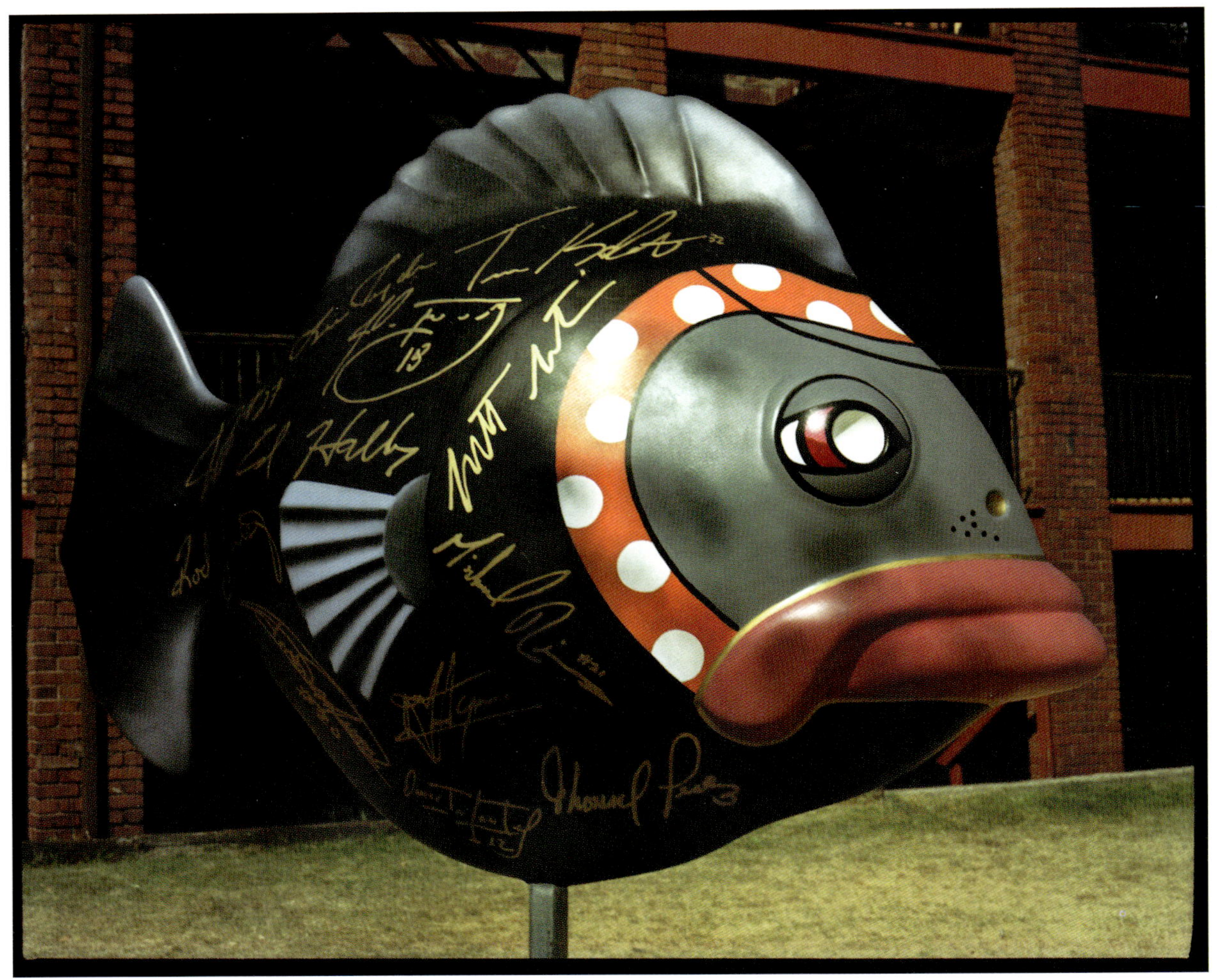

AutograFish
artist: Tom Potocki
patron: Erie Seawolves
location: 110 East 10th Street

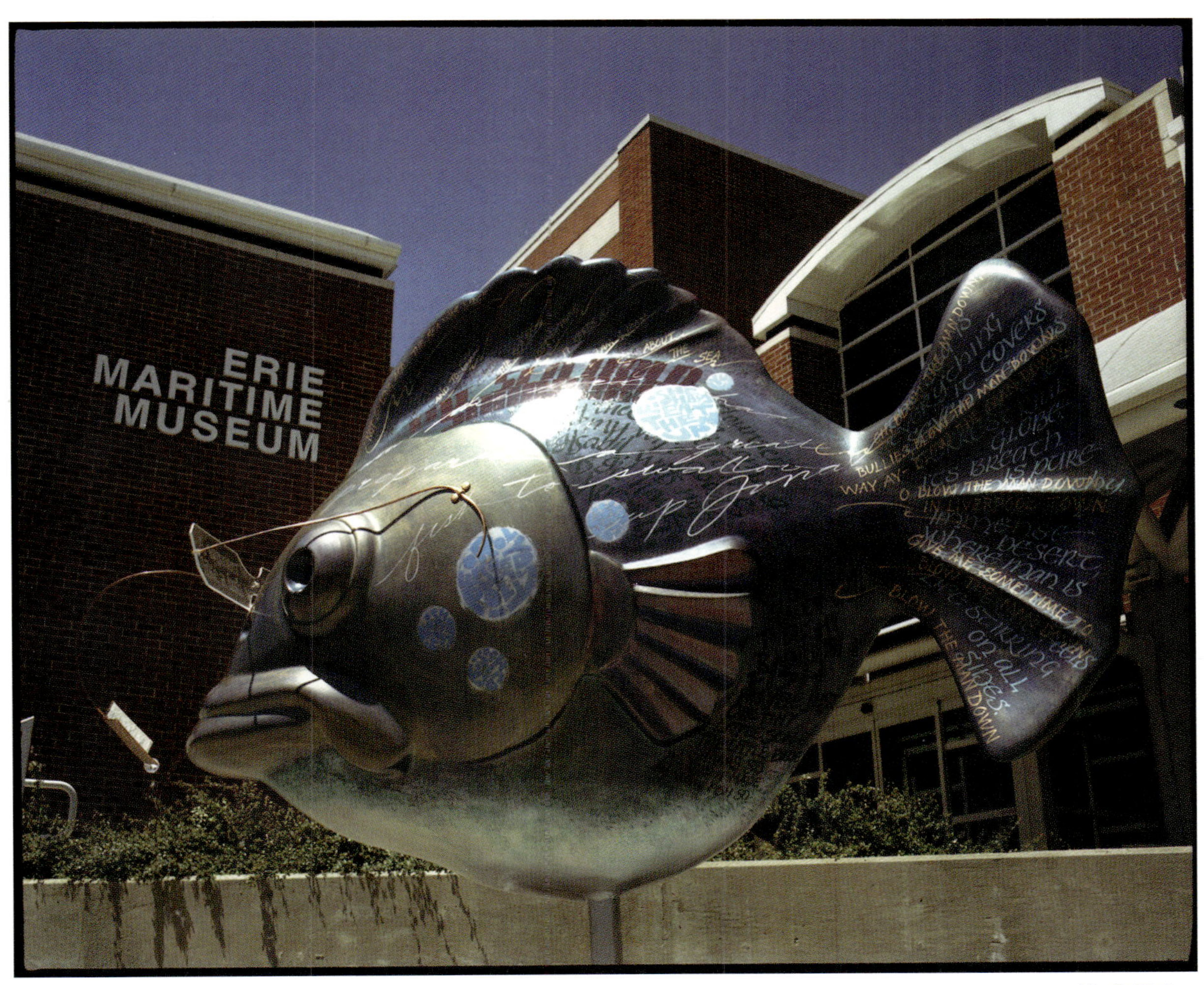

Fish Tales

artists: Jodi Staniunas Hopper & Toni Kelly

patrons: Alice Novotny, Italo Cappabianca, Sue Sutto, Erie Maritime Museum, home port of U.S. Brig Niagara, & Dr. Jeffery & Carol Renz Blake

location: 160 East Front Street

How To Prepare a Splash of Pollock

by Chef Patrick Rodgers of Crowley's Restaurant

Pick up Splash of Pollock in 1967 Ford Country Squire Wagon. Transport to Polish Falcons Club where Mrs. Stankiewicz, Mrs. Godzwa and Mrs. Wisnewski can chop, cut and filet him. Then, knowing these ladies like I do, they will take a two-beer-and-two-cigarette break, return to the kitchen and beer batter the pollock filets. They will then run the fish as an evening special with cole slaw and potato pancakes for $2.95.

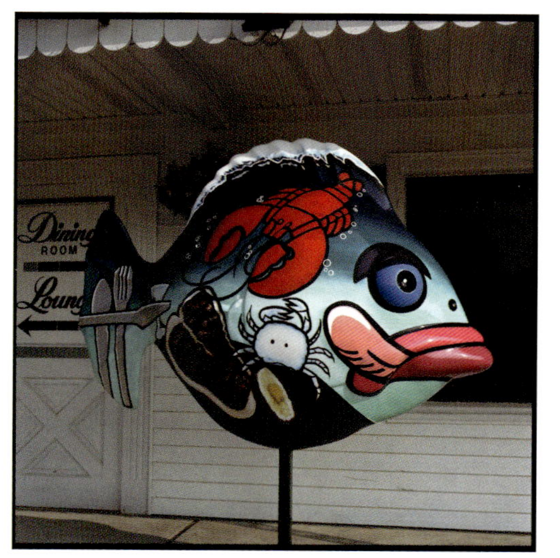

Blue Eye Sole
artist: Jack Parks
patron: Colony Pub & Grille
location: 2670 West 8th Street

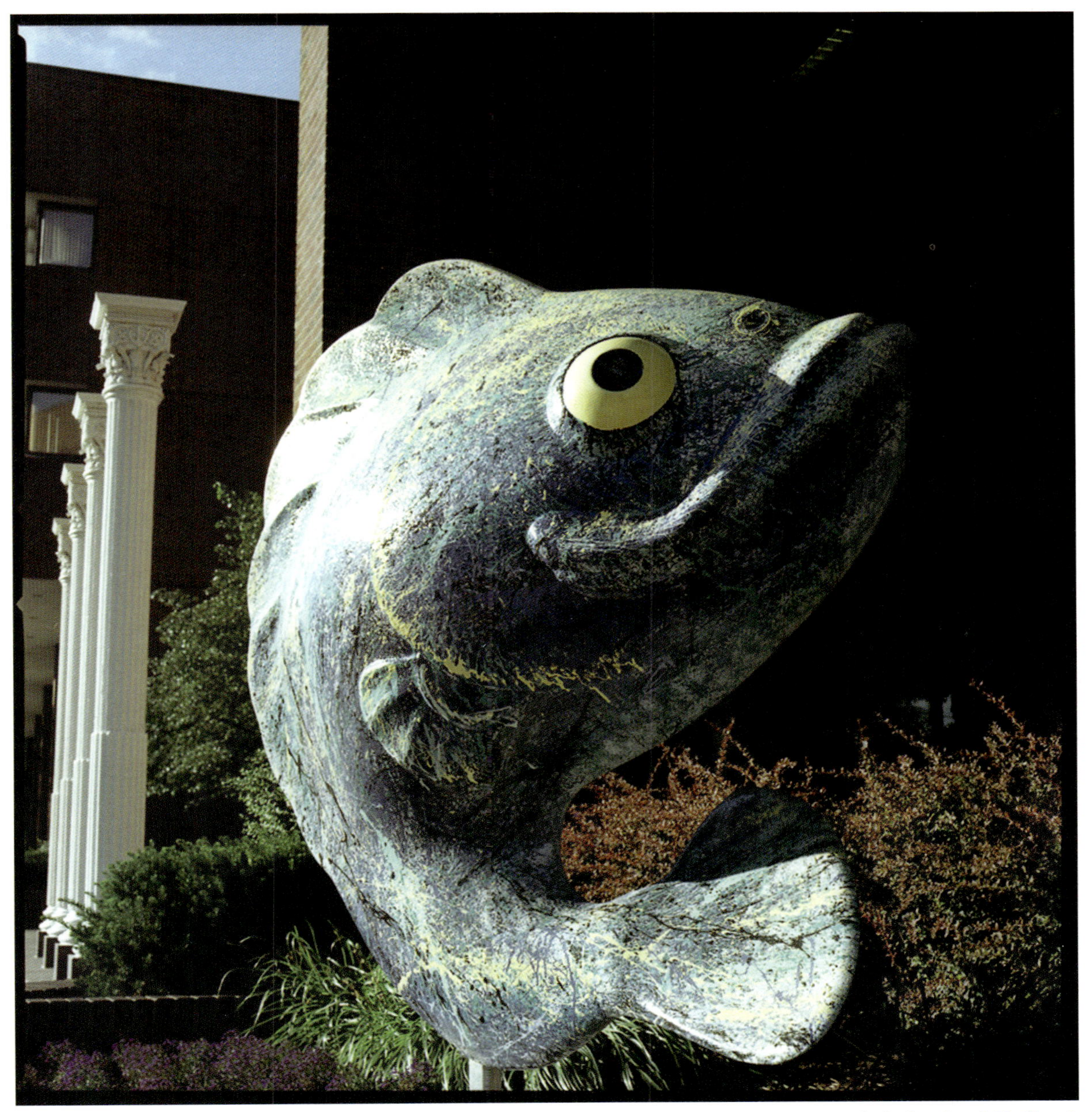

A Splash of Pollock
artists: Erie Insurance Corporate Design Department
patron: Erie Insurance Group
location: East 6th & French Streets

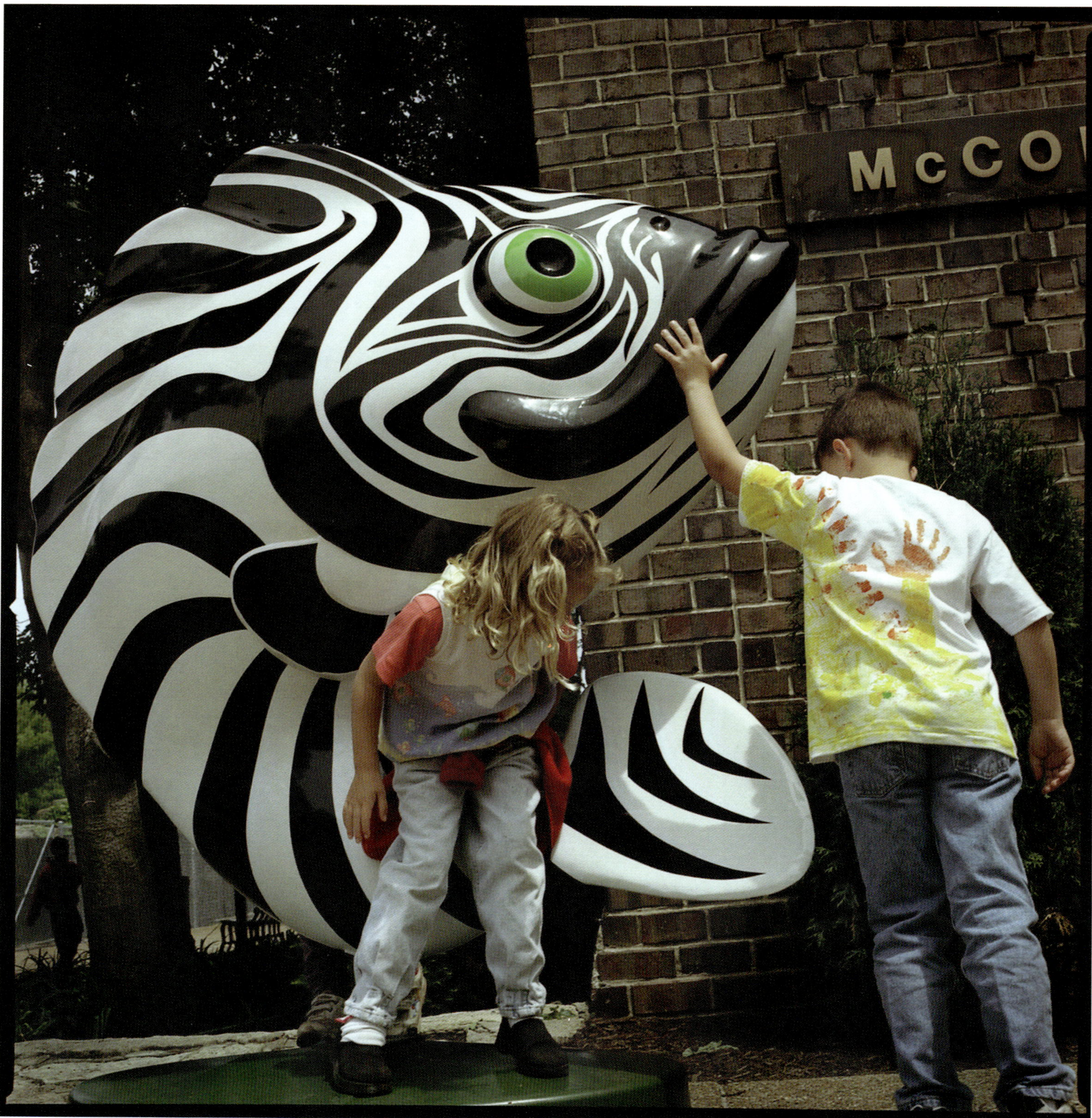
McCO

Blackened Whitefish
artist: David N. Seitzinger
patron: The Fish Commish
location: Lincoln Park Zoo, Chicago, IL

onasadnote

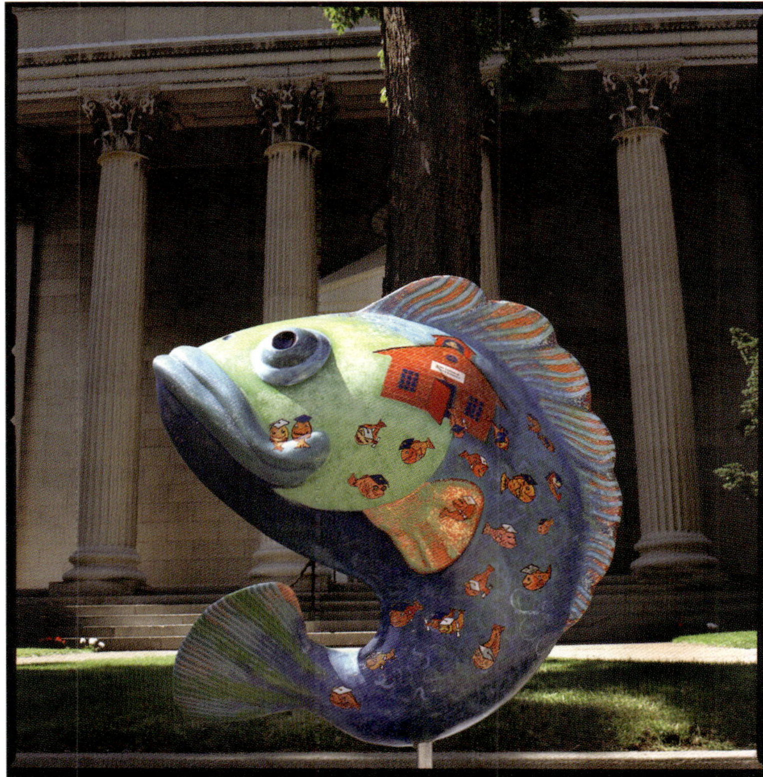

Schoolin
artist: Evelyn Askey-Zaleski
patron: Fort LeBoeuf School District, Evelyn Askey-Zaleski Scholarship Fund
location: 130 West 6th Street

Evelyn Askey-Zaleski passed away during the summer of GoFish!, after a lengthy illness. Memorials were requested to go to a scholarship fund in her name in care of the Ft. LeBoeuf Foundation

Fish under construction when *GoFish!: The Offishial Tale* went to press: Bad Bass Biker, artist: Karen Larsen, patron: Alek Powersports and Chocolate Covered Bassberry artist: Bill Hanna, patron: Romolos Chocolates/Tony Stefanelli.

fishbegetfish...

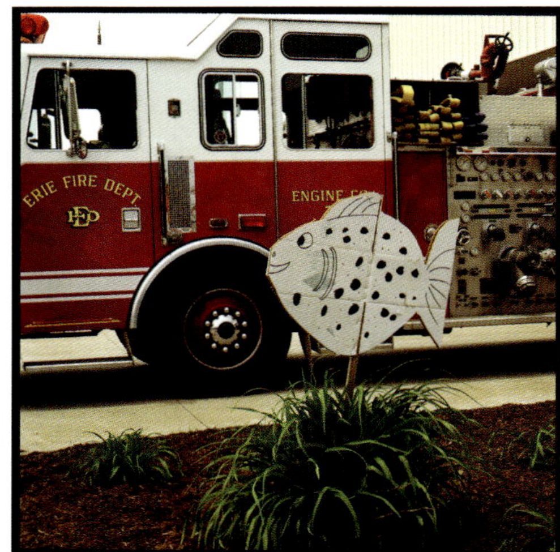

If we've learned one thing in the summer of 2001, it's that. For every GoFish! fish that dove into the Erie streets, many more were spawned in the forms of homemade pins, t-shirts, hats, and more. Creativity was flowing higher and faster than the waves in the bay!

Unoffishial fish showed up on business signs, in front yards and on advertisements. Firemen created a Dalmatian Fish, made of a white cardboard box, outside their station house. A pizza shop lacking the dough for an offishial fish showed their support by painting a pizzafish on its State Street window— pepperoni and all. And 10-year-old Louise Wiest, who was sad after cutting 12 inches off her hair and donating it to Locks of Love, created the plywood "Glitzy Glamour Fish" with her parents, who suggested it as a way to cheer her up. It is covered in sequins, jewels and glitter with big red lips, and holding court on their lawn each day.

They say that imitation is the sincerest form of flattery...and we're *thrilled* that this proved true with GoFish!

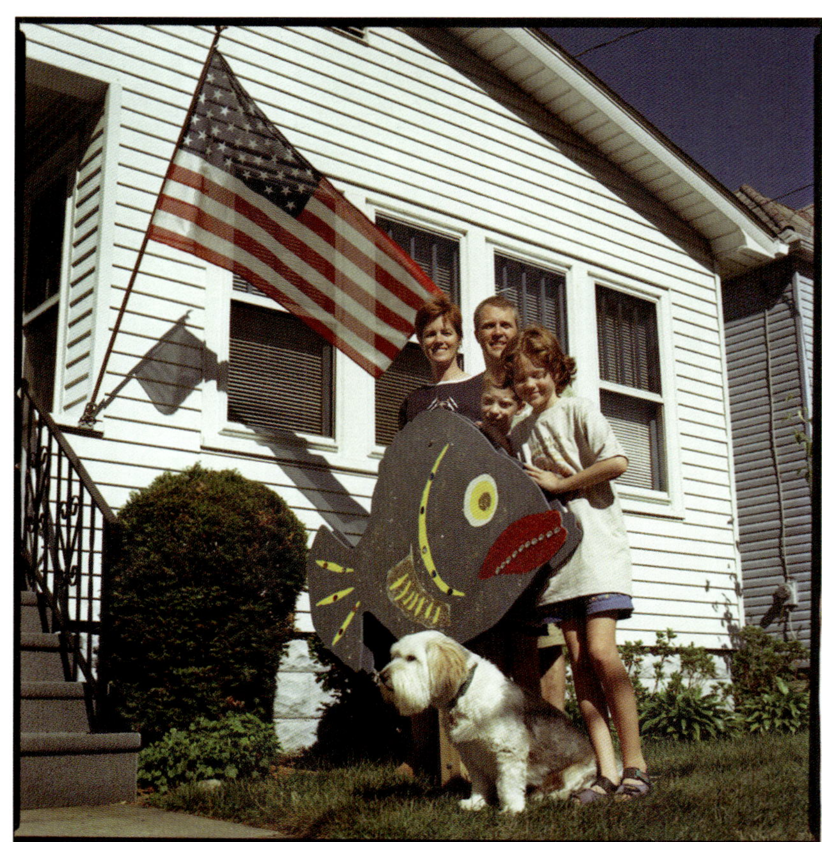

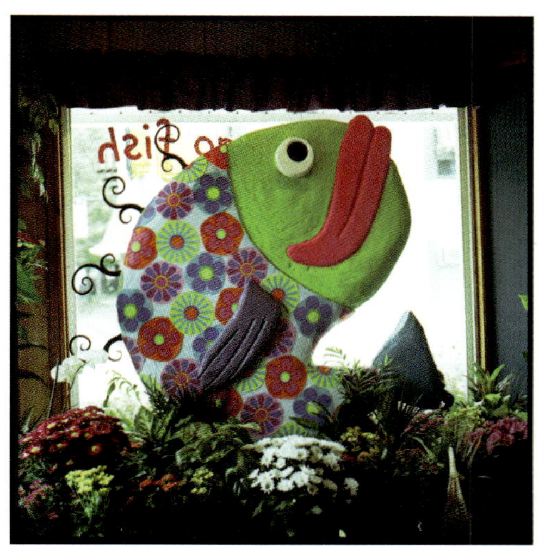
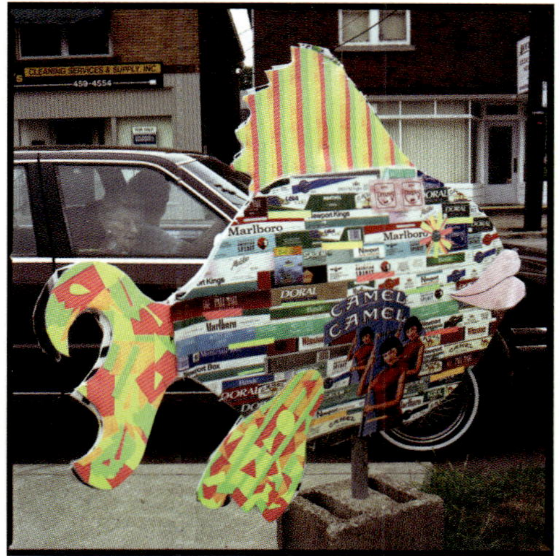
CLEANING SERVICES & SUPPLY INC.
Marlboro
Marlboro
DORAL
CAMEL
CAMEL
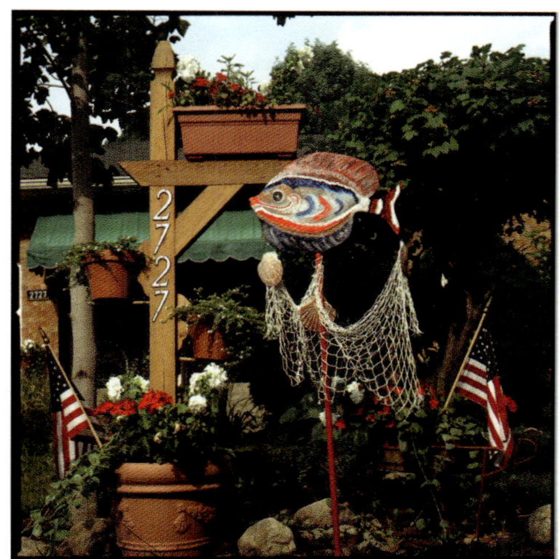
2727
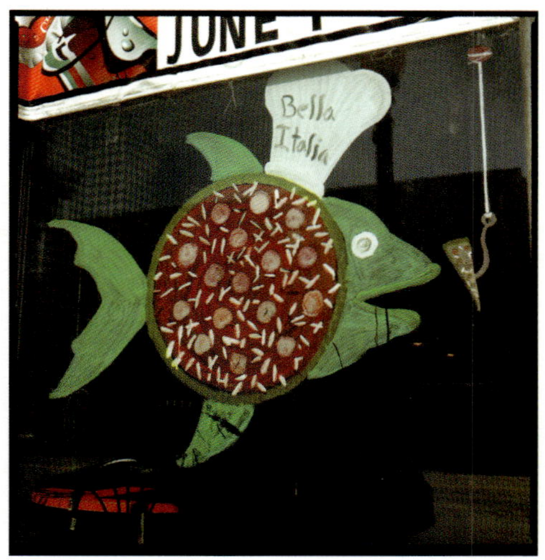
JUNE
Bella
Italia
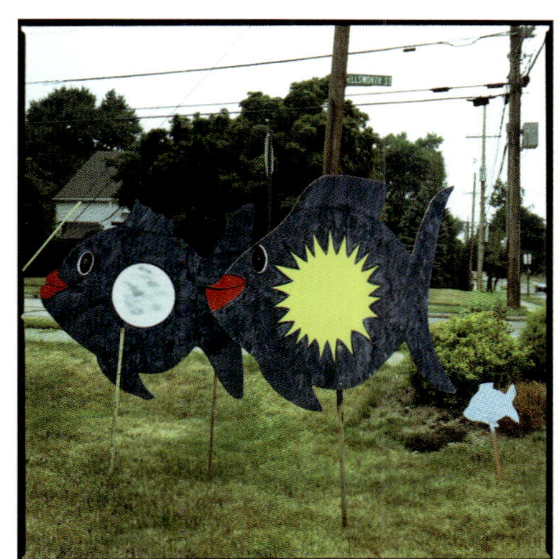
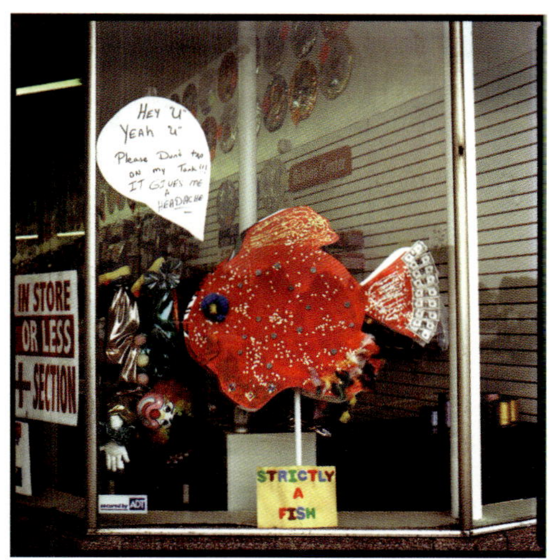
Hey "U"
Yeah "U"
Please Dont tap on my Tank!!! IT GIVES ME A HEADACHE
IN STORE
OR LESS
SECTION
STRICTLY
A
FISH
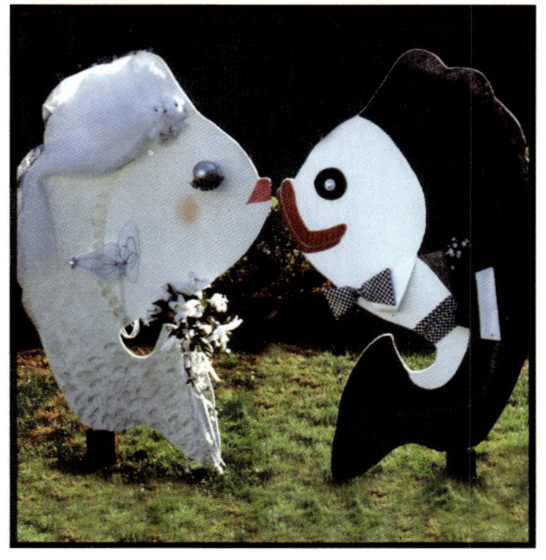
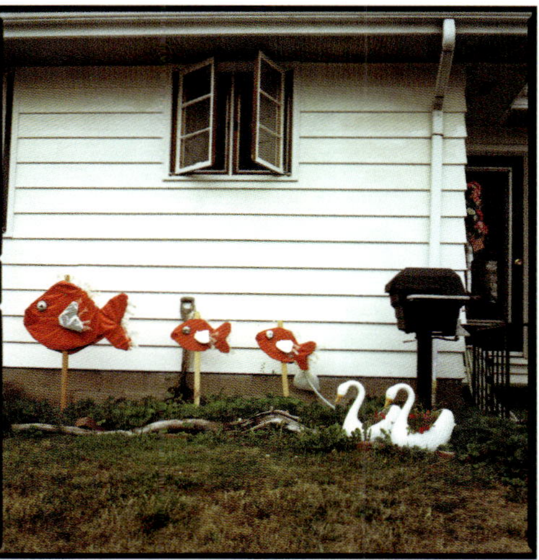
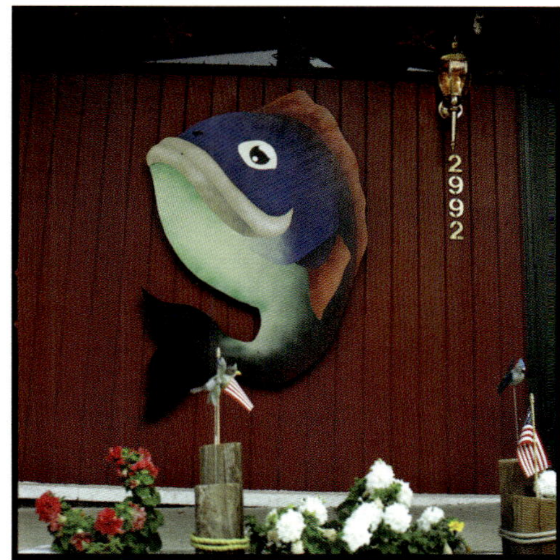
2992

fishonfish

We were thrilled to the gills!
J. Bradley and Mary M. Gill

It was wonderful to see something in Erie, where a lot of people, young and old, can enjoy together...we've enjoyed taking lots of pictures.
Donna Finn

We were "lured" to seek out the colorful works of art. They caught us— hook, line and sinker! What a wonderful summer project.
Wayne and Phyllis Pollock

Erie's colorful fish swim from bay to upper State St., to every compass point, turning our town into an open air aquarium.
James R. Finn ("Jim Finn")

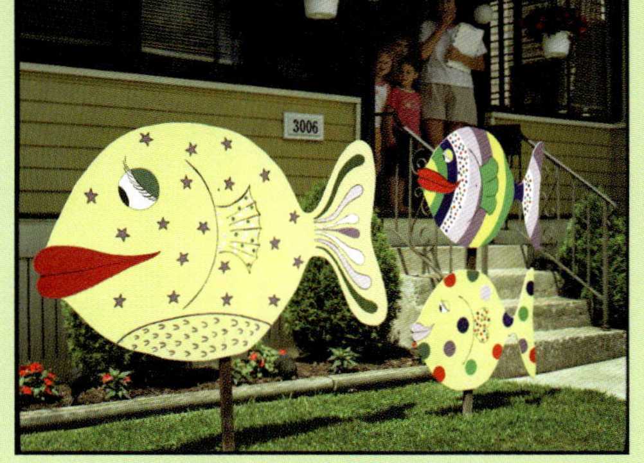

Fantastic— interesting— spectacular—
honestly creative, you bet.
The most beautiful fish I ever met.
Something I really like— and my name is
Alice Mae Pike

Colorful fish all over Erie.
Beautiful, bright— they're never dreary.
Creative, "cool"— they make us cheery.
Those fantastic fish all over Erie!
Whether Bass, Pollock, Salmon, or King,
We all agree GoFish! is the thing!
So much talent Erie's artists bring.
All over town, their praises we sing!
Louisa P. Salmon

Our children rode around town with their Grandma Joyce to see them. They were thrilled by all of them.
Mr. & Mrs. Patrick H. Finn

Each fish is a treasure to the Erie area. The talented artwork displayed on each fish is extremely beautiful! We are proud to share our name with these wonderfully "fishy" creations!
Timothy and Tina Fish & family

We loved it! My two youngest grandchildren and I took a day to see the fish and then went out to dinner together. Tyler is 8 and Katie is 6.
Mrs. Oliver L. Finn

It's easy to be hooked, each one has a different look. Every fish you see is one of a kind, each one has a unique design.
Cindy Pike

After years of endless "Fish" nicknames— Tuna, Filet-O-Fish, Goldie, etc.— it is refreshing to have the GoFish! extravaganza create fun and appealing names like Sturgeon General and Bad Bass Rider that *all* fish can be proud of! We have truly enjoyed the entire "fishy" project. Great work!
Jack and Karen Fish

Working at the Bicentennial Tower, we got a daily view and feedback from the public on how well this went over.
Monica Finn

Erie's GoFish! are just like caviar from the Sturgeon General and Dr. Sturgeon— the quintessence of class!
Nancy J. Sturgeon

On a "scale" of 1 to 10, us Fishes give it a 10!
Gary & Sue Fish, and Megan & Adam

All our friends asked if we sponsored a fish, or had one named after us. Unfortunately not!
Douglas and Delly Fish

I think the phish are phantastic!
Sylvia T. Gill

We think the fish are wonderful and give so much credit to the people who took part in Erie's GoFish!
John and Jeanne Finn

fishspeak

The more the fish appeared, the more we all talked about the fish. The more we talked about the fish, the more we lapsed into FishSpeak. So if you can't get enough fish....

parts of speech

Noun: There is the fish. I see a fish. Which is your favorite fish?

Verb: I like to fish. You're fishing for compliments.

Adjective: That's a fishy story. I smell a fishy smell.

Adverb: I'm feeling fishy today. Your story sounds rather fishy to me.

Interjection: Fish! I dropped the bowling ball on my foot!

Preposition: He walked up, headed fishward, and then went into the library.

usage in everyday speech

We're up to the gills in fish paraphernalia.

It's just fin-tastic.

On a scale of one to ten, the fish are a sixty-three.

Holy mackerel, is this GoFish! thing fun.

I detoured on porpoise, just to see Baked Fish.

I'm floundering around, trying to get photos of all of them.

Albacore-ming to see you, just as soon as I finish looking at fish.

Tuna 'twait for me; I'm going to look at Sexy Sadie a bit longer.

I'd like to have the halibut, just for the halibut.

Perch chance you'd like to join me for shrimp on the barbie this evening?

I can't seem to find that last fish. My map-reading skills are quite crappie!

It's all atrout the fish this summer.

Salmon chanted evening, I should go see Glow Fish in the dark.

It takes about an hour to go pike-riding around the peninsula.

Walleye just *love* GoFish!

I need to head up to the Mall, and mako see Dr. Utley's fish on the way.

Can you go fish-finding with me tomorrow? Shark-can!

It's offishial! GoFish! is making a splash!

The project is coming along swimmingly!

We're waiting with bait-ed breath to see what's next for Erie's art community!

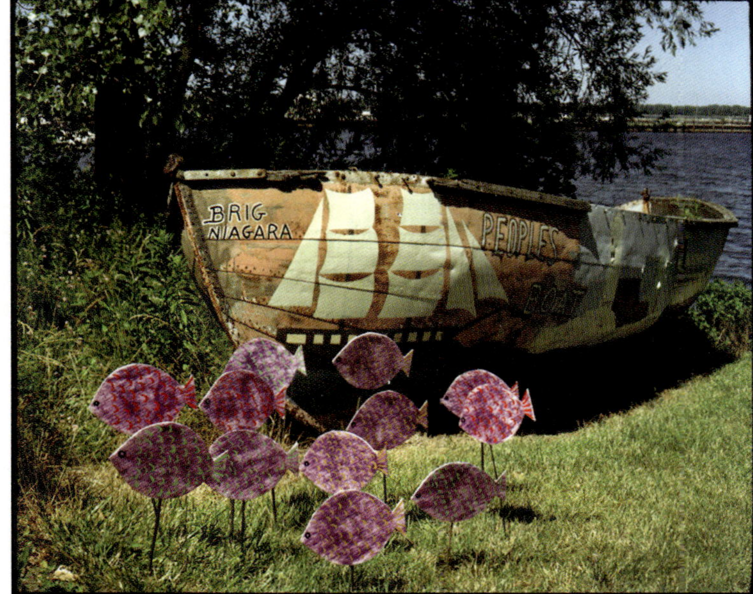

We've been lured in, and have fallen hook, line and sinker for GoFish!

fishsongs

Sea Eeled With A Kiss

That's a Moray

Clam Every Mountain

It Haddock Be You

Shark! the Herald Angels Sing

Fiddler Crab On The Roof

You Walrus Hurt The One You Love

Sole Train

Heart And Sole

Nearer My Cod To Thee

Roe, Roe, Roe Your Boat

I Never Smelt This Way Before

fishmovies

Marlin Rouge

Jurassic Carp

The Blair Fish Project

Pulp Fishin'

Silence of the Lemmings

The Codfather

Cast Away

Titanic

Home Abalone

Forrest Guppy

Jaws

Waterworld

Happy Gill-more

funwithfish

It's not just a coffee table book, it's a big square coaster! It's not just a photographic compilation, it's a slice of Erie history, a capsule in time, a celebration of the summer of 2001! And hey—when it's done being all those things, it can be just plain fun.

When you're not busy looking through the wonderful photos, or arranging it at just the right strategic angle on your coffee table to impress visitors, here are some ways you can use this book—for party games!

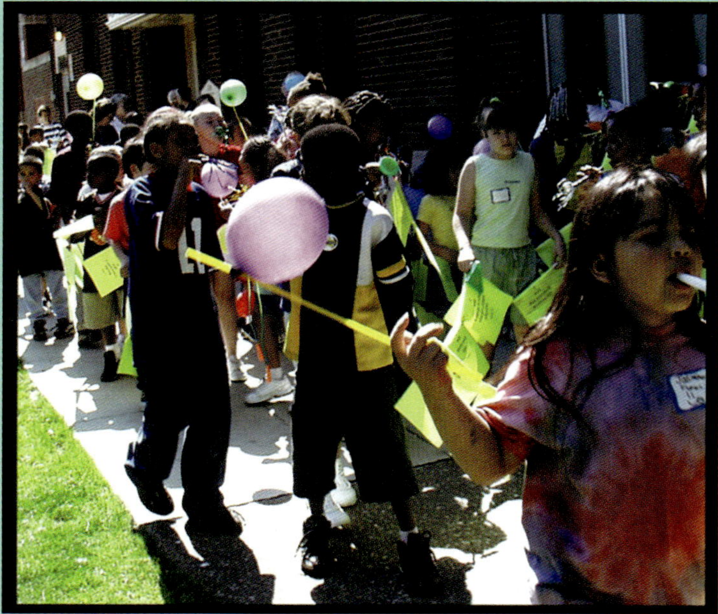

So round up your family and friends, and dive into the following thought-provoking cod-versations:

1. **What's your favorite fish, and why?**
2. **What's your least favorite fish, and why?**
3. **If you were a GoFish! fish, which one would you be, and why?**
4. **If you could create your own fish, what would it look like?**
5. **If you could bring one of the GoFish! fish to life, which one would it be, and why?**
6. **If you had to eat one for dinner, which one would be tastiest? Why?**
7. **If it were brought to life, which GoFish! fish would be the smartest? the funniest? the most likely to succeed? most likely to become President? most likely to appear as a Playfish centerfold?**
8. **If you could play matchmaker and set up two fish on a date, which ones would they be, and why? What would their date involve?**
9. **Which fish is most likely to be Future Mayor of Erie, and why?**
10. **Play Twenty Questions with the fish, and have others ask yes/no questions until they figure out the answer ("is this fish wearing a bikini? does it have propellers? is it horizontal?")**

note: A typical GoFish! party would include fish-related offerings such as Swedish fish candy, goldfish crackers, fish-shaped cookies and the like. If it's a more upscale affair, you might consider something like smoked salmon, caviar, and chocolate mousse done up in a copper fish mold. It doesn't really matter what you serve, though, because *anything* can be transformed into fish fare with a bit of creativity and determination. Plain old spaghetti becomes Long Skinny Fish Swimming in the Red Sea! Chocolate pudding is considered Lake Erie in November At Dusk! And jellybeans turn into Sugar-Encrusted Orbs of Rainbow Trout.

The Fish Commish

Co-Chairs:

- **Jody Farrell**
  Tungsten Creative Group
- **Mary Alice Doolin**
  SDF School Program IU #5

Project Advisor:

- **Susan Black-Keim**
  Gannon University

Committee Members:

- **Tom Bergdahl**
  American Express
  Financial Advisors
- **Diane Blake**
- **Angela Brooks**
  Gannon University
- **Geri Cicchetti**
  Erie Times-News
- **Pamela Graham**
- **Doreen Foutz**
- **Susie McAllister**
- **Alice Novotny**
  MailWell Print Group
- **Vanessa Paris**
  Highmark Blue Cross Blue Shield
- **Nancy Potter**
  Composiflex
- **Marne Roche**
  Rice Realty
- **Tammy Schell**
  Hamot Health Foundation
- **Nicole Smith**
  Erie Art Museum
- **Cindy Stadler**
  Gannon University
- **John Vanco**
  Erie Art Museum
- **Ronee Yasher**
  Gannon University student

Special thanks to:

All the artists and patrons who have made this such a special event and....Mark Dombrowski and Marlene Mosco at PNC Financial Services Group; Mark Rendulic and Jim Gehrlein at National City Bank; David L. Seitzinger, David N. Seitzinger & Cindy Seitzinger; Cindy Duda, Jana Hunt, Steve Schillo, Mike Wellington, Jerry Fisher, Fred Showalter, Joy Armbruster, Gary Garnic and Don Gunter at Gannon University; Joe Weunski at Tungsten Creative Group; Jim Lynch, Jamie Potosnak, Eran Hakanen, Jen Reinhardt, Andrea Sertz, Amy Schulz, Ruth Lynch, Stacy Corapi, Mike Richwalsky, Damon Kleps, Georgia Baggs, Sandy Holland, Chenoa Seay & Leslie Stewart; Jeff Biletnikoff & Carrie Smith at CyberInk; The staff of the Erie Art Museum; Karen Duska-Martin; Tim Rohrbach of Rohrbach Photography; Denise Keim; Tom Farrell & Zach Hess, Nigel T.; Joe & Kathy DeAngelo; Mike Paris, Matthew Brooks, Matt Roche, John Vahanian; Paul Frazer; Gary Cacchione of Dovetail Gallery; John Bucklin; Leslie McAllister; Jack McAllister; Dale Pierce; Osiecki Brothers; Nancy Senger, Sheila Hultgren, Jackie Swanson, & Janet Sherr (The Unveiling Party Committee); Gary Schneider, Robin Fahey, Tom Pontillo, Sr. at Howard Industries; AJ Grack, Rich Niejelski, Anthony Grack and Joe Bires, at AJ Grack Interiors; Dave Brugger, Mel Burdine, Larry Huston, Scott Burdine, Robert Miner, Greg Fisher, Jamie Beatman, Rich Milligan, Frank Peterson at Horton Precast Concrete; Bill Schwartz, Bob Lilley, Robert Schwartz at Star Mobile Homes Supply; Mike Geer, Mike Sjostrom, Jerry Bender from Molded Fiber Glass Companies; Mark Kukla, Char Markiewicz, Jeff Spaulding from the City of Erie; Mayor Joyce Savocchio; County Executive Judy Lynch; Rubye Jenkins-Husband and City Council; Bill Correll at the Avalon Hotel; Dave Chrzanowski at Gohrs Printing; Jennifer Reed and Terri Reed Boyer at Relish; Gary Spurgeon and Regent Communications: WXTA Country 98, Classy 100, & WRIE AM 1260; Scott Brooks, Chris Brooks and Sean Brooks; The staff of the ExpERIEnce Children's Museum; Casey Miller; Annita Andrick of the Erie County Historical Society.

indexoffish

Fish under construction when *GoFish!: The Offishial Tale* went to press:

Bad Bass Biker, artist: Karen Larsen, patron: Alek Powersports

Chocolate Covered Bassberry artist: Bill Hanna, patron: Romolos Chocolates/ Tony Stefanelli

fishyawards

GoFish! is full of fabulous fins and tails, gills and scales. Chosen by a volunteer Awards Committee, these awards are scattered throughout the book. All fish that weighed in by the book's publication deadline were considered in at least one category, sometimes more. To spread the glee, no fish could win more than one category. The committee toiled and struggled in deciding GoFish's tastiest fare, and in the end, wishes it could award every single fish, for each is a catch of the day in its own way!

people'schoiceawards

These awards were given to the fish that collected the most votes from our online voting ballot at **gofisherie.com.**

Sources:

Rothermel, Jim. "Musical Fish Puns." http://www.jimrothermel.com FishJokes.htm.(29 Aug. 2001).

"Bouillabaisse." http://users2.ev1.net/~jeduke/ss003.htm. (31 Aug. 2001). Whitman, B.

Nelson's Biographical Dictionary and Historical Reference Book of Erie County, Pennsylvania, Erie, Pa.: S.B. Nelson, 1896.

Frew, D. & MacDonald, R.J. (2000). *Home Port Erie: Voices of Silent Images*. Erie, Pa.: Erie County Historical Museum.

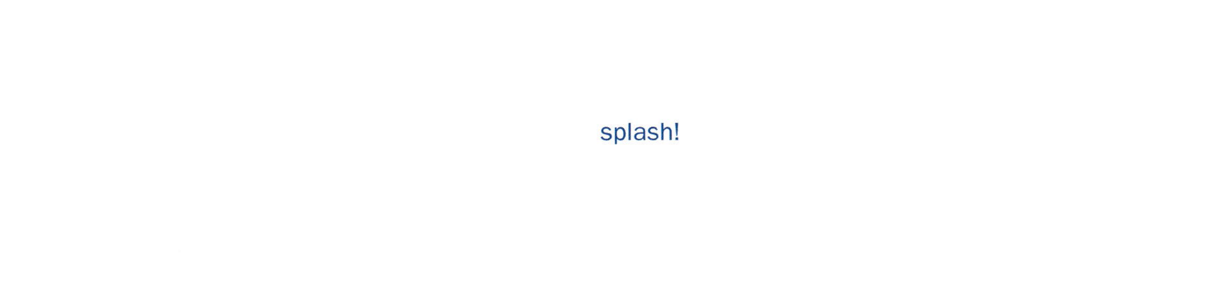

splash!

juicy sushi red haring
swingin' in the rain fis
night swimming refle
fathom five when you
andiamo pescare elfis
suede fins flying fish
sunset sturgeon genera
and red (fish) all ove
house fair gilled lady v
fishtorical perspective
autografish stocks an
ziegfeld flounder su
fishheads alo lost on
whitefish red, white an
halibut patricia fisha th
fish red fish blue fish